KING EMPEROR'S JUBILEE

1910  1935

by

F. G. H. Salusbury

The extracts from Queen Victoria's journal and correspondence are quoted, by permission, from "The Letters of Queen Victoria," published by John Murray.

Bibliography : "The Reign of King George the Fifth" by D. C. Somervell (Faber and Faber), "King George and the Royal Family" by Edward Legge (Grant Richards), "The Crown and the Kingdom, England's Royal Family" by Colonel R. J. Blackham (Sampson Low), "Queen Mary" by Kathleen Woodward (Hutchinson), "George V, King and Emperor" by E. Major (James Nisbet), "Monarchy" by Sir Charles Petrie (Eyre and Spottiswoode).

Art Editor, Ivor Castle

*

DAILY EXPRESS PUBLICATIONS
LONDON, 1935

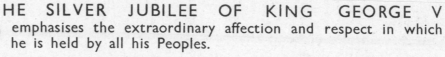

THE SILVER JUBILEE OF KING GEORGE V

emphasises the extraordinary affection and respect in which he is held by all his Peoples.

No other constitutional monarch could deserve these tributes in such full and heartfelt measure. The repository of universal trust, he is, in the twenty-fifth year of his reign, the very essence of the unity of the British Commonwealth of Nations.

His reign has covered not only the age of scientific miracles, but the greatest war in history and a period of unparalleled unrest. Institutions and traditions, morals, philosophies and religions, have everywhere been attacked by humanity in a delirium of doubt. Systems of government and statesmen have been called to account and declared bankrupt. Unemployment has inspired world-wide misery and resentment.

Yet, in this Empire the bonds have never been closer between King and people.

The radicalism, the questioning of authority, which Napoleon remarked regretfully on his return from Elba, developed simultaneously with the grandiose procession of wealth and surface prosperity that moved through the years of the 19th Century. They broke into clamour after the accession of George V.

Queen Victoria had been regarded with almost mystic veneration. Edward VII—the "uncle" of Europe, beloved "Teddy" of the crowds—had exercised superlative charm in a short, socially brilliant reign. In 1910, a Prince of Wales, whose personality was lost in that of his father and grandmother, succeeded to the leadership of a nation on which long delayed storms burst in bitter fury.

It was soon evident, however, that this captain knew the right course. He approached the crew as man to man, without shedding one whit of the dignity of his office. He made them realise that he and his wife desired most sincerely the happiness of all other men and their wives.

He brought the ship to harbour for repairs by virtue of those qualities which receive least publicity but which are the foundations of happy family life—selfless devotion to duty, high purpose in all things, understanding of his fellow men, and a simple honesty of character.

History may well rate the King as the greatest statesman of his time. It is certain that the man who does most to make the world safe for democracy sits to-day upon the British Throne.

F.G.H.S.

The Boy who became King

King George's childhood and early manhood. He comes in direct succession to the throne with the death of the Duke of Clarence, and marries Princess May of Teck.

CHAPTER ONE

GEORGE the Fifth, by the Grace of God, of Great Britain, Ireland and the British Dominions beyond the Seas, King, Defender of the Faith, Emperor of India, was born at Marlborough House on June 3, 1865, the second son of the Prince and Princess of Wales.

There seemed no prospect of his ever bearing the majestic titles which are his to-day. He grew up happy and carefree, the "pickle" of the royal family. When he was in Ceylon, in 1882, one of his partners at a dance asked him if he would like to be heir-presumptive to the throne.

"I'm jolly glad I'm not!" he replied. "My brother has to receive all the kow-towing on this tour round the world, and has a rotten time, while I lark about and enjoy myself. We're

THE KING.
In Field-Marshal's Uniform.

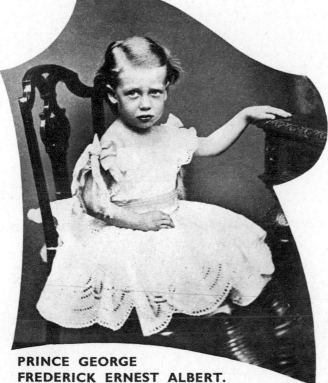

PRINCE GEORGE FREDERICK ERNEST ALBERT.
The Royal "pickle" at the age of two years.

stopping at Government House now, you know, and old Wait-a-bit-Jim—" his nickname for the Governor "—button-holes Eddy by the hour, and never bothers about me."

Responsibilities at an early age.

Ten years afterwards "Eddy," the Duke of Clarence, was dead, and a great responsibility descended on his grief-stricken younger brother.

The first news of Prince George, apart from official announcements, appears in a letter written by Queen Victoria to the King of the Belgians on June 8, 1865 : "Alix is recovering extremely well, and the child is said to be much larger than little Albert Victor, and nice and plump. Bertie seems very much pleased with this second son."

"Bertie" and "Alix" were the Prince and Princess of Wales, afterwards Edward VII and Queen Alexandra. Albert Victor was the Duke of Clarence.

On June 13, Queen Victoria wrote to the Prince of Wales concerning the baby's names : "My dear Bertie . . . I fear I cannot admire the names

**QUEEN VICTORIA WITH HER DAUGHTER-IN-LAW
AND GRANDCHILDREN.**

Prince Albert Victor, later Duke of Clarence, whose tragic death in 1892 brought his younger brother into direct succession to the throne, is on the left, with his hand resting on the lap of his mother Alexandra, Princess of Wales. The Princess of Wales' left arm is round the waist of Prince George. Sitting on Queen Victoria's lap is the future Princess Royal, Duchess of Fife.

you propose to give the Baby. I had hoped for some fine old name. Frederick is, however, the best of the two, and I hope you will **call** him so; George only came over with the Hanoverian family. However, if the dear child grows up good and wise, I shall not mind what his name is. Of course you will add **Albert** at the end, like your brothers, as you know we settled **long** ago that **all** dearest Papa's **male** English descendants should bear **that** name, to mark **our line,** just as I wish all the girls to have Victoria at the end of theirs! I lay great stress on this; and it is done in a great many families."

Eventually he was christened George Frederick Ernest Albert: and the Queen herself came quite happily to call him "Georgie."

His Royal Grandmother's opinion

The Queen's first impression of her new grandson was that he "is very small and not very pretty, but bigger than Albert Victor—who is a dear little fellow—was at that age."

As time passed it became evident that he shared at least one quality with his august grandmother: he knew his own mind, and showed that he did.

PRINCE GEORGE
as he was when he entered the Britannia training ship.

THE CLOSE RESEMBLANCE
between the boyish Duke of Clarence (bareheaded) and his mother can be seen in this picture, taken in 1877.

" HIS SMILE IS SINGULARLY SWEET."
Prince George, seated, with his brother and sisters. Princess Louise (Princess Royal) is on the left. Princess Maud (the Queen of Norway) is next her, holding her hat in her right hand. Princess Victoria, rather conscious of the photographer, is on the right.

His fancy had been so taken by an under-nurse, who bathed him occasionally, that he decided to be bathed by no-one else, and announced his decision with howls. They were such convincing howls that his decision was parentally confirmed.

Another story of his early childhood exemplified him as the supreme "pickle." His conduct in the presence of Queen Victoria was once so exuberant that she told him to go under the luncheon table until he was good. There followed a most decorous silence for some ten minutes. He was then asked if he had repented. He said cheerfully that he had. "Very well," said the Queen, "you may come out."

The last thing she could have expected to see appeared. A tiny pink figure, gurgling with laughter, crawled over the carpet. Prince George was as naked as a cupid. The decorous silence had been devoted to taking off his clothes as a pleasant surprise for his elders.

A natural disposition on all occasions

A photograph of his brother, his sisters and himself, taken about 1873, shows him as the most natural of the group. The others have retained some of the stiffness in which they were posed. Prince George is sitting at his ease and looks straight into the camera. His smile is singularly sweet—just that smile with which a million angelic children habitually veil meditation on an especially fiendish prank.

He was attracted early to a sailor's career. The late Sir Richard Holmes said—"I was Royal Librarian when King George was a boy, and gave him books to read. He preferred those which treated of naval subjects." Then—and with what echoes of one's own childhood!—"He liked to paint the engravings, even those in editions de-luxe, giving the coverings of a horse a green tint, and painting a cow red and an elephant yellow."

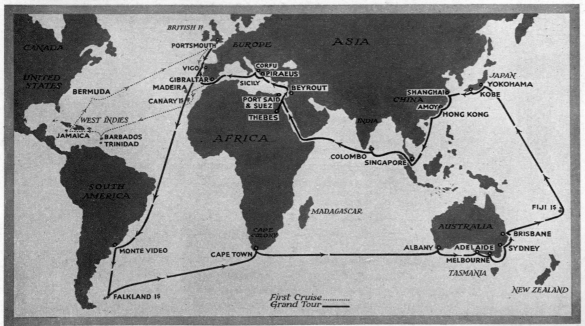

THE CRUISES OF THE BACCHANTE

In 1879, Prince Albert Victor ("Eddy") and King George set out to see the world. Their first voyage took them to the West Indies. The main voyage covered South America, South Africa, Australia, Fiji, Japan, the East Indies, Ceylon, Egypt and Palestine. They returned home in 1882.

THE DUKE OF CLARENCE AND KING GEORGE

in Highland dress. The King was then nine years old.

A Royal Family Party at Osborne House

In the nineties of last century. Official dispatch boxes cover Queen Victoria's table. Queen Mary is seated on the left, with the Prince of Wales, in a white sailor suit, in front of her, and the Princess Royal on her knees. King George, then Duke of York, has his hands on the shoulders of the present Duke of York. Others in the group are the late Duchess of Connaught, seated on Queen Victoria's left, Prince Arthur of Connaught, and the Queen of Spain (Princess Ena) in a large white hat.

Her Majesty Queen Mary

CHILDHOOD

GIRLHOOD

THE FASHION FOR 1887

THE FIANCÉE OF THE DUKE OF YORK

"May, who looked very sweet." A charming picture of Princess May of Teck, taken in 1893.

QUEEN MARY'S PARENTS
the Duke and Duchess of Teck.

KING EDWARD'S FAMILY.

A Marlborough House group in the last years of Queen Victoria's reign.
Left to right : the Duke of Clarence, the Queen of Norway, Queen Alexandra,
the Princess Royal (Duchess of Fife), King Edward (then Prince of Wales).
Seated : King George and Princess Victoria.

The Prince of Wales, who had overwhelming recollections of his own education, was convinced that his sons would benefit most from a naval training. The discipline, which bred self-reliance, the healthy life, the chance of seeing the world with the minimum of royal etiquette—nothing could be better for boys whose later years would be rigidly circumscribed by their rank.

Both brothers went to the Britannia training ship at Dartmouth in 1877, and, two years later, began those voyages round the world in the Bacchante which was the foundation of King George's knowledge and appreciation of the British Empire. They first visited the West Indies,

where the dockyard slums at Port Royal, Jamaica, inspired them with such horror that they thought the Government should buy them and burn them. Many years later the younger brother, then Prince of Wales, was to show this characteristic impatience with slackness in his "Wake up, England !" speech.

Crossing the "line," in 1880, towards South America, the Princes were properly ducked by Neptune. It was the sort of fun which Prince George, especially, liked. He was the more robust of the two, the fatter, the rosier cheeked. Prince Albert Victor ("Eddy") was the quieter, the dreamier. They were known, however, to their

THE FINEST ROYAL RESIDENCE IN THE WORLD.

The immemorial home of Kings and Queens seen from the
air. Saint George's Chapel is in the foreground.

messmates as "Herring" and "Sprat," names which knew no difference of temperament.

The squadron which included the Bacchante was suddenly sent to South Africa on the outbreak of the first Boer war, but the Princes saw no active service. They then sailed to Australia, where they went down mines, hunted Kangaroo, and saw as much of the country as they could. One curiosity was the home-made armour worn by Kelly, a desperate "bushranger," or bandit, who had been shot the year before. Prince George tried it on and found that it weighed ninety-seven pounds.

Ready for adventure

On the voyage from Melbourne to Sydney Prince George recorded in his diary—"at 4 a.m. the Flying Dutchman crossed our bows." That was an adventure of the right kind. The phantom ship was seen by thirteen people—"a strange red light shone out ahead and in the midst of it, outlined quite vividly, were the masts, spars, and sails of a brig coming up on the port bow and not more than two hundred yards distant. The midshipman ran forward, but, before he reached the forecastle, the spectral ship had vanished. The night was clear, the sea was calm, and it was possible to see right away to the horizon. No explanation of the phenomenon was ever forthcoming."

KING GEORGE
The Bridegroom.

One wonders if this was a practical joke played by the Prince on his diary, for he is credited with many others. There was the sub-lieutenant whose cot he filled with marline-spikes : and there was the super-refined medical officer, addicted to afternoon tea, on whose cabin door he painted the notice "Ladies Only."

Maternal devotion

Both boys adored their mother, whose beauty was the shrine of a completely lovely nature. Prince Albert Victor was extraordinarily like her, and there was the closest sympathy between them. A youthful acquaintance of his recorded that "his intense devotion to her touched me, young and careless as I was. He showed me a letter of hers he always carried, and kissed it before he put it back in his pocket."

The temperamental difference between the brothers is indicated by a remark made to the same person by Prince

AN ESPECIALLY GRACIOUS PICTURE OF QUEEN MARY
in court dress in the reign of Queen Victoria.

THREE GENERATIONS OF THE ROYAL HOUSE

King Edward VII is seated between his son, King George V, and the Prince of Wales, then a naval cadet.

14

THE BRIDAL GROUP OF KING GEORGE AND QUEEN MARY

Among King George's decorations may be seen the Order of the Thistle, which was one of Queen Victoria's wedding presents to him.

ADMIRING QUEEN MARY'S WEDDING DRESS

It was of white satin, with a silver interwoven design of roses, shamrocks, thistles and orange flowers.

George. "Eddy and I often have awful rows," he said, "and we go for each other like two turkey-cocks. You'd think he gives himself airs, but he's a much better boy than I am, and my mother worships him. Isn't she, my mother, beautiful?"

The Bacchante went on to Fiji, and Japan, where the Princes were presented to the Emperor and attended a military review. Prince George was particularly interested in the efforts of his superior officers to master the lively ponies on which they were mounted. He had fun, too, watching the Japanese tattooers practice their art on his shipmates, and is said to have had a dragon done on his own arm. At the same time he had a long talk with the Japanese Minister of the Imperial Navy. He was fascinated by the new Japan which he saw emerging from its medieval skin.

In China, whose villages impressed him with their "awful stinks," he got some mixed shooting up the Wusung River from Shanghai—so mixed that, one day, he brought down a pheasant with his right

HORSE TRANSPORT UNVANQUISHED.

The Strand as it was in the days of hansom cabs and tall hats. All the buildings
on the left have gone. Somerset House looms high on the right.

Their Majesties
at a Fancy Dress Ball

YORK COTTAGE, SANDRINGHAM

Built as overflow quarters for bachelor guests from Sandringham House, it was the first home of the King and Queen. Five of their six children were born here.

THEIR FIRST BORN

barrel and a deer with his left. This was prophetic of the skill he so developed with gun and rifle as to be recognised as one of the best shots in his Empire.

The Princes returned to England, which they reached in August 1882, by way of Singapore, Ceylon, Egypt and Palestine. In the dawn, outside Jerusalem, Prince George woke to hear sparrows chirping, and said it made him think of home. This simplicity of his is discovered early in his jokes, his love of life, and his concern with deeper things. It amounts to the entire lack of affectation which has always been his and which confounds every cynic—to the sincerity which is exemplified in a promise made to his mother in 1881, and kept ever since, that he would read daily a chapter of the Bible.

Queen Victoria found "Eddy" very tall on his return—"a great deal taller than Bertie, very slight. Georgie is also much grown, in fact, more in comparison, though there is still a great difference between the two. He has still the same bright merry face as ever." Prince Albert Victor now entered the Army as an officer in the 11th Hussars, but Prince George continued his sailor's career, gaining promotion in the usual way and in no sense as a privileged

THE KAISER AT PEACE

King Edward is on the left. Then come the Kaiser, Queen Alexandra and King George. The Royal children are the Princess Royal, the Duke of York, the Duke of Gloucester, holding his father's hand, and the Prince of Wales.

royalty. He showed seamanship of a high order, as the commander of Torpedo Boat 79, when he towed a disabled sister ship to safety in a heavy storm. The Prince, who was promoted to the rank of Commander in 1891, was a thoroughly efficient officer. The whole-hearted approval of the Senior Service is not easily won, but, throughout his life at sea, Prince George was affectionately regarded as a man who knew his work and loved it.

An important change in the prince's life

On January 14, 1892 his life was ruthlessly changed by the death of his beloved elder brother, the Duke of Clarence. Prince George was now in direct succession to the Throne. His naval career had to be abandoned. The following May he was created Duke of York, Earl of Inverness and Baron Killarney.

The Duke of Clarence had been engaged to Princess May of Teck, of whom the German Emperor said—"a handsomer and more accomplished young princess is rarely to be found," She was a great-granddaughter of George III, through her mother, who was a daughter of the Duke of Cambridge, younger brother of George IV. She was thus an English princess, and the Duke of York's engagement to her in 1893 was extremely popular. The match was of their own choice. There was never any doubt of that, any more than there had been of a similar freedom in the engagement

QUEEN AND EMPRESS

Queen Mary driving through Berlin with the late Kaiserin

IN ALL HIS GLORY

The Kaiser and King George, wearing German uniform, riding to a
review of troops in Potsdam.   The year before the Great War.

of his sister, Princess Louise, who impetuously told Queen Victoria that she would rather die an old maid than not marry the Duke of Fife.

The Queen Mother's consent to the engagement

Queen Victoria wrote in her journal for May 3, 1893 : "Received a telegram from Georgie from Sheen House to say he was engaged to May Teck, and asked for my consent. I answered that I gladly did so. I wrote to him also by a special messenger. Saw Sir H. Ponsonby, and arranged that the news should be put in to-morrow's papers. I have so much wished for this engagement that it gives me the greatest satisfaction."

The wedding, having been fixed for July 6, in the Chapel Royal, St. James' Palace, the Queen wrote on May 8 : "Saw dear Georgie at one, and talked over all the arrangements. It is a pleasure to do so with him as he is so sensible,"—the supreme virtue in Her Majesty's estimation.

Wedding Presents

On July 5, after recounting the presents she gave to Princess Mary—"the Victoria and Albert Order, a handsome diamond necklace, stuffs and shawls, Indian and others, and a fine flounce of old lace which had belonged to Queen Charlotte" —the Queen says : "Dear Georgie came, and I gave him the Order of the Thistle. He gave me a dear little diamond brooch, with his and May's cypher, and a coronet and two anchors. Rested a little."

FROM CADET TO ADMIRAL
The King, as Prince George (left) with the Duke of Clarence : and reviewing his fleet at Spithead.

KING EDWARD'S DERBY TRIUMPH

His Majesty is obviously delighted with the cheers of the huge crowd that saw the victory of his horse Minoru, in 1909. He is between Mr. Richard Marsh (hatless), the Royal Trainer, and Lord Marcus Beresford. King George is on the right.

Wedding Preparations

She had need of all the rest she could take, for the wedding day was "overpoweringly hot." While the Queen was dressing "Mary (herself very handsome)"—this was the Duchess of Teck—"brought in May, who looked very sweet. Her dress was very simple, of white satin with a silver design of roses, shamrocks, thistles and orange flowers interwoven. On her head she had a small wreath of orange flowers, myrtle and white heather, surmounted by the diamond necklace I gave her, which can also be worn as a diadem, and her Mother's wedding veil."

The Ceremony

The Queen proceeds—"May was supported by her father"— the Duke of Teck—"and her brother Dolly"—Adolphus, first Marquis of Cambridge. "Georgie gave his answers very distinctly, while May, though quite self-possessed, spoke very low. The music was well played and sung, but sounded weak and inferior to that in St. George's Chapel. I could not but remember that I had stood where May did fifty-three years ago . . . May these dear children's happiness last longer !"

The Queen though "very tired" was very happy. The marriage was an ideal one. The wedding arrangements had been perfect. She concludes her journal on that day with a note on the "very fine illuminations" and the "enormous crowds" that were out.

May's pleasing disposition

The Duke of York, now twenty-eight years old, was facing the beginning of his most arduous and selfless public life. But he had a helpmate whose qualities were destined to enrich the meaning of wife and mother, and whose example has always inspired society and the family alike.

"We all had tea together on the terrace," recorded Queen Victoria, at Osborne, at the end of July, "and then I drove alone with May, who was so nice, and quite at her ease, indeed a very dear girl. She talked so pleasantly and sensibly."

IN THE BUTTS AT BOLTON

AN EXPERT SHOT
King George shooting pheasant and wild duck at Brocket Hall

The Duke
and Duchess of York

A new life of public duty takes the place of King George's naval career. His visit to Australia inspires his memorable "Wake Up, England!" speech. With the accession of Edward VII, he is created Prince of Wales.

HIS FAVOURITE PASTIME
The King happy to be aboard his yacht Britannia

CHAPTER TWO

THE popular ignorance of the Duke of York—as King George was to remain until he became Prince of Wales in 1901—seems curious to us who feel that we know the Royal Family so well to-day. He had, of course, to shoulder all those responsibilities which would have been the Duke of Clarence's, to be on view, on parade, as the eventual heir to the Throne. But three causes combined to keep him in comparative obscurity—the tremendous presence of his grandmother, the glittering personality of his father, and his own modesty, his own sense of the proprieties of his life.

A new title—and his duties

If we can consider "proprieties" in its true meaning of things which are fitting, and so strip it of the smugness with which it has been invested by an age hostile to tradition and lacking practical moral foundations, we may come to a working sense of the King's attitude. Primarily he is a man with a conscience. He knows what is right, what is wrong. He does his duty. His duty, then, as Duke of York, was to assist and obey his grandmother and father just as efficiently as he had served his superior officers in the Navy. And all his training was to do it as unobtrusively as possible.

Even so, it is astonishing to come across a description of him written in 1908 which asserts that he "entirely lacks what may be called the Hanoverian curiosity, the insatiable desire to know and see everything. He has no craving for long journeys and sightseeing, being generally content to survey the surrounding country from the golf links." There could hardly be a more fatuous misconception of his character than that—and it was written only two years before he became king.

No use for favourites

The writer, however, was completely accurate in the following paragraph :—"Like his grandfather, Prince Albert, not only has his name never been mixed up with any scandal, nor, indeed, associated with the name of any

The King's Coronation Pr

...ession entering Whitehall

25

THE CORONATION OF GEORGE THE FIFTH

The scene in Westminster Abbey just before the crown was placed on the King's head.

woman save his wife, but he has shown himself strictly adverse to choosing his favourites among the rather—well, shall I say, rich upstarts and merely rowdily amusing vulgarians and sycophants who are ever playing for royal recognition."

York Cottage, Sandringham

The married life of the Duke and Duchess began in York Cottage, Sandringham, which had been built as quarters for an overflow of bachelors from Sandringham House. It now was a home, and there, with the exception of the present Prince of Wales, all their children were born.

The Cottage stands on a lawn, some little distance from the House, surrounded by fine trees and overlooking a narrow lake. It is an unpretentious building, two-storeyed, sprouting with chimneys and bay-windows. In this home, which the rowdily amusing vulgarians mentioned above would probably condemn as inadequate for the swinging of their cats, the young couple found that "extraordinary delight in each other" which has never failed ; that "marked preference for each other's company which explains why, in the early days, King George always bounded up the stairs, and before he reached the top you could hear him : 'May, where are you ?' Always came the same reply : 'I am here.' "*

For eight years their life followed practically the same routine. They moved to York House, St. James' Palace, for the "season." They went to Windsor and Scotland. They came back as a family to York Cottage for Christmas.

An extra wing of bedrooms was built on in 1901, for the presence of five children had made more space imperative. Edward Albert Christian George Andrew Patrick David was born on June 23, 1894 ; Albert Frederick Arthur George, on December 14, 1895 ; Victoria Alexandra Alice Mary, on April 25, 1897 ; Henry William Frederick Albert, on March 31, 1900 : and George Edward Alexander Edmund, on December 20, 1902. John Charles Francis was born on July 12, 1905 and died on January 18, 1919.

Family Life

The Duke of York, in those last years of the nineteenth century, was quietly experiencing the normal happiness of a husband and father in a normal British home. This is the fact which his contemporaries either overlooked or took so much for granted that they forgot it ; This is the fact which, as he grew older in years and happiness, governed

Crowned and Robed

The King and Queen on the Balcony of Buckingham Palace, after the coronation.

his increasing contacts with his future subjects, and which accounts for his unrivalled position to-day—the wise, good head of a family looked up to with affection by families all over the world.

His Children's Welfare

If he had adopted some fantastic theory of education for his children he would have gained the temporary publicity which is accorded to cranks. He proceeded, however, in the ordinary way which is dictated by common-sense. The children regarded him as the supreme authority in their lives, but as one who had delegated to their mother all control over their early upbringing. In other words this father and mother occupied precisely those places in the childish scheme of things which Nature has indicated as being most healthy and the best possible insurance against the production of little prigs.

The father never allowed any questioning of the mother's authority, and, in this connection there is a story of the present Prince of Wales who had been told by his mother on one occasion that he must not go out into the grounds. He wanted to go very much. Resentment bred a bright idea. He went to his father, who knew nothing of the ban, and made his request as if it were completely novel. He got permission : but, when he returned, it was to find that his plot had been discovered and to face punishment of the sort which the law majestically calls condign. He attempted no more tricks of that sort.

Cool and determined

The Duke of York was now becoming expertly acquainted with the management of a country estate. His reputation as one of the best shots in the United Kingdom was establishing itself. He has a style of his own with the gun. All good shots have. It is said that he once asked another famous shot what he thought of it. "Well, sir," replied the other, "frankly I think it is rather awkward." "I thought so myself," said the Duke, "but, you see, it suits me, and I intend to stick to it."

It may be pointed out, however, lest the merely stubborn take heart, that he always made sure of the excellence of the things he stuck to. Another story credits him as remarking that he had great respect for a motto which he had learned in the Navy— "Keep your hair on !" These two stories, in conjunction, illustrate his character perfectly. A long time afterwards it was reported that he recommended the motto as advice

* " Queen Mary," by Kathleen Woodward

THE KING AND HIS GUARDS

No man is less than 6 ft. 2 in. in height. The tallest is 6 ft. 5½ in. A striking picture of the King's Company of the 1st Battalion, Grenadier Guards, on the terrace at Windsor Castle. The King, in the centre of the first row, is wearing his uniform as Colonel-in-Chief of the Regiment.

for those empurpled Tories who nearly burst at the contemplation of Mr. Ramsay MacDonald as Prime Minister of the National Government.

A Favourite Sport

Recognised to be one of the prettiest shots in the country, he once performed the extraordinary feat of "firing both barrels of two guns in such rapid succession that he had four pheasants falling through the air at the same moment." At Balmoral—with the rifle—he achieved "what is nearly a record—out of twenty-two stags, the result of a week's stalk, he had thirteen to his credit."

The last decade of the nineteenth century seems, in retrospect, to have something of the glamour of a series of summer afternoons. It was the period of enormously puffed sleeves for women, of deer-stalker caps for men, of black waistcoats worn in the evening with white ties and tail coats, of Japanese fans as wall decorations, of bows tied on the legs of chairs, of a frock-coated gentility in commerce, of the bicycling craze with Mayfair a-wheel in Battersea Park—"Daisy, Daisy, give me your answer, do!" And the storms that were on their way were rumbling below the horizon.

IN THE DUCHY OF CORNWALL
The King and Queen returning from a visit to the Phoenix tin mines.

MR. BALDWIN buys a rose in Downing Street

Alexandra, <u>the</u> Rose Queen

—So does MR. LLOYD GEORGE

—and MR. RAMSAY MACDONALD

The young Kaiser Wilhelm was playing with a new toy—the Imperial German Navy. He had been in raptures, quite childish raptures, over his appointment as Admiral in the British Navy. He felt that his own navy must be superior even to that of his "dear Grandmama," and his ambition was so successful that we, ourselves, were hurried into progress and improvement. Perhaps he realised he could never rival Frederick the Great as a military figure. But he saw that the oceans were wide open to him. He made impressive visits to Cowes, always irritating his temperamental uncle the Prince of Wales, but regarded, one suspects, with good-humoured tolerance by his first cousin, the Duke of York, whom no one could teach anything about the sea.

Our self-satisfaction was jarred also in South Africa, where the second Boer War broke out in October 1899. It had one good effect in that the Army, too, was inspired to reform. We learned that the leisurely, glossy tactics of a military tradition which, though never deficient in courage, opposed good-breeding to professional enthusiasm, were useless against a determined enemy who did not play the game as taught in the great public schools and the hunting-field. The apocryphal remark of the Hussar subaltern, who said that the function of cavalry in modern warfare was to give tone to what would be otherwise a vulgar brawl, was an echo of a large part of the military mind at the end of the last century.

31

DISEMBARKING
FOR AN
IRISH VISIT, 1897

THE KING
AT LORD'S, 1914

It was considered absurd by the staff that these upstart South African republics could give the British Army a moment's trouble, and, in that spirit, the war began. The troops—officers and men—did their jobs as they had been taught, but were soon badgered into bewilderment. Gradually we became cleverer, but only after much hardship and some shocking reverses.

The fact that we were organised into an Empire was, perhaps, brought home for the first time to the people of these islands by the contingents, especially from Australia, Canada and New Zealand, which joined in the Boer War. The growth of the British communities was also emphasised by the federation of the Australian States into a Commonwealth, an achievement which was proclaimed on January 1, 1901.

"SO YOU'RE THE KING!"

A happy incident of the Royal visit to
Sunderland in 1918.

BALMORAL CASTLE
THE KING'S
SCOTTISH HOME

AS COLONEL-IN-CHIEF
OF THE BLACK WATCH

A MEETING WITH HIS
GRAND-DAUGHTER
PRINCESS ELIZABETH

34

Queen Victoria died three weeks later, her last years made tragic by the War, but it had been her wish that the Duke of York should represent her at the opening of the first Federal Parliament of Australia. She knew, just as did her son—now Edward VII—and her grandson, the importance of the crown as the rallying point of the world-wide British peoples : and the departure of the Duke and Duchess of York in the liner Ophir, specially manned with a crew from the Royal Navy, on March 16, was a hopeful sign in a year of gloom.

They sailed by way of the Suez Canal, touching at Gibraltar, Malta, Port Said and Aden. They made a brief tour of Ceylon and then, after a visit to Singapore, they reached Melbourne, where the Duke performed the ceremony of opening Parliament—incidentally, during one morning in Melbourne he shook hands with four thousand people—and was able to see a great deal of the continent, considering the time at his disposal. From Australia the Duke and Duchess went to New Zealand, Mauritius, South Africa—where the war was still in progress—and finally to Canada and Newfoundland. He had covered some fifty thousand miles and seen seventeen British possessions. No other member of the Royal Family had gained so wide an experience of the Empire.

The Duke's Humour

There are many anecdotes of the tour of the Duke and Duchess of York—that, for example, of the Australian official who kissed the Duke's hand with such devotion that he was for ever afterwards known by the nick-name of "Kissie." There was the delightfully formal signal made by the Captain of the Ophir to the escorting ships Juno and St. George after the ceremony of "crossing the line" had been completed—"His Royal Highness noticed that the main braces of the Ophir, Juno and St. George, required splicing and hopes this may be done this evening." For the benefit of the uninitiated, "splicing the main brace" is a liquid rite still observed in the Navy and is practically equivalent to "wetting one's whistle."

The Duke and Duchess were the centre of innumerable official functions. They reviewed troops. They saw picturesque native ceremonies in Australia, New Zealand and Canada. The majestic salute of kneeling elephants in

LIVES WHICH ARE CLOSE TO THE QUEEN'S HEART

The Sex War for Women's Suffrage

AN EARLY COMBATANT
IN ACTION

MRS. FLORA DRUMMOND, ARRESTED
IN HYDE PARK, 1914

MRS. PANKHURST, ARRESTED
OUTSIDE BUCKINGHAM PALACE, 1914

THE DERBY TRAGEDY OF 1913
Miss Emily Davison, a suffragette, threw herself in front
of the King's horse, Anmer, and was killed.

THE BOYS AND GIRLS—AND THE KING—
ARE OUT TO PLAY

Ceylon, the thunder of vast mobs of beasts rounded up on the cattle stations of Australia, the rhythmic crash and stamp of a Maori war dance, the presentation of decorations to soldiers in South Africa, the vast plains, mountains and forests of Canada—with its Red Indian chiefs and flourishing French civilization in Quebec as two of the more divergent aspects of humanity which owed allegiance to the British Crown ; all these were colourful memories of the tour. The most important thing which remained, however, was a new Imperial consciousness, coupled with unmistakable evidence that the Duke was far in advance of the insular spirit which animated a great many of his fellow countrymen.

Prince of Wales

He had become Duke of Cornwall on the accession of Edward VII, and on November 9, 1901, he was created Prince of Wales and Earl of Chester. It was as Prince of Wales that he made the most memorable speech of his career at the Guildhall on December 5, 1901. The text was "Wake up, England!" and it passed at once into a slogan. It was another shock ; and a most salutary one to the worship with which British merchants and manufacturers, drugged with recollections of past glory, had so long regarded themselves.

Not only was it an excellent tonic speech, but it was delivered with a sincerity and vigour which put the Prince of Wales at once in the forefront of public speakers. It is said now that he has a perfect broadcasting voice—every word he says can be heard distinctly, every inflection is right—and that was true literally and metaphorically of his words in the Guildhall thirty-four years ago.

His first public speech

As with his shooting, he had developed his own style of oratory. The old Duke of Cambridge had proffered him advice when he had to make his first public speech. "Have your speech printed, hold it in your hand," said the Duke "and refer to it when the moment comes." The young prince neglected this veteran advice and, while he was speaking, without notes, he heard the Duke exclaim

The Princess Royal
Shortly before her fifteenth birthday

"Conceited boy ! why doesn't he do as I told him. He is sure to break down." But he did not break down, and his speech was a great success.

On this afternoon at the Guildhall it was the Prince of Wales' turn to give advice, and its very position towards the end of a more or less formal account of his tour added to the force with which it struck his hearers. It was the last thing which an official audience had expected to hear from the heir to the throne. He was telling them how to get on with their work. The cheers which he aroused came from a delight that was electrified with surprise.

"To the distinguished representatives of the commercial interests of the Empire," he said, "whom I have the pleasure of seeing here to-day, I venture to allude to the impression which seemed generally to prevail among their brethren across the seas, that the old country must wake up if she intends to maintain her old position of pre-eminence in her Colonial trade against foreign competitors." It was on this note of prescience and of profound appreciation of the common cause which binds the mother country and the overseas Dominions together that the new Prince of Wales took up his position in public life.

The things which he said had all been waiting to be said, but no-one apparently had thought them worth saying until the heir to the throne voiced what was, after all, the opinion of all sensible men.

Family re-union

He had done invaluable work as the representative of the Crown. Now he resumed his comparatively obscure role as the son and heir of his far more spectacular father. He resumed, too, that family life which he had always cherished. It had been a terrible wrench for him and his wife to part from their children. The joy of being re-united to them was all the greater from the moment when their frantic waving was seen as the Ophir put in to Portsmouth. A new century had been born, and with it a new idea of the mutual responsibilities of all the British peoples. That was directly the work of the Prince of Wales.

MOTHER AND SONS
The Queen with the Duke of York and (right)
the Prince of Wales.

The King's Coronation Drive through

London—Passing the National Gallery

CROWNED AND ROBED FOR THE DELHI DURBAR, 1911

42

Storm Clouds over Europe

The new Prince of Wales establishes himself in high estimation at home and abroad. His visits to Canada, India and Europe.

CHAPTER THREE

THE reign of Edward VII, considered after the tremendous events of the last twenty-five years, has a fantastic air of unreality. Somewhere a monstrous Nero was fiddling while the foundations of European civilisation burned away beneath him.

Never was diplomatic intrigue more active ; never was society more lavish, more ostentatious, in its display of wealth and luxury ; never was there such a general dicing with fate.

King Edward, popular as he was, shrewd, witty, the man of the world personified, had periods of profound melancholy. Sometimes he felt himself an old man in a crazy world. He saw the path that his nephew, the German Emperor, was taking, and loathed its implications. In an especially depressed mood, he thought of abdicating. He had worked passionately for peace. The Entente Cordiale of 1904 was directly to his credit, and put an end to that period of Anglo-French hostility which had been marked so recently by the almost hysterical reception of President Kruger in Paris. What was to become of all the work of Edward the Peacemaker ?

His Father's confidence

His son and heir was his greatest hope. King Edward was a penetrating judge of character. The frequently quoted remark that is attributed to him—"My son will reign, but not my grandson"—was really the highest tribute he could pay to the Prince of Wales who is now George V. It meant that his son could ride out the approaching storms, if anyone could. Beyond that he saw nothing.

The Prince of Wales was enriching his reputation of being the first member of the Royal Family to delve into the factories and living conditions of the industrial masses of the people with all the zeal of a Government inspector : and with a great deal more than that—with all the sympathy of a warm-hearted man. His one object, in work and relaxation, was to know the truth about his future subjects. It was because he succeeded so thoroughly that he came, after the Great War, to be the one permanent value in a market of crashing creeds.

ACCLAIMED BY INDIA
The King-Emperor and Queen-Empress present themselves to their people

KING-EMPEROR AND QUEEN-EMPRESS
AT DELHI, 1911

44

INDIA'S PRINCELY PAGES

in attendance on the Imperial balcony

The Royal Tour of India and Burma, 190

DRIVING THROUGH
THE KHYBER PASS

THE QUEEN RETURNING FROM A RIDE

46

The King and Queen, then Prince and Princess of Wales, watch elephants at work in a Burmese timber yard.

IN PROCESSION ON STATE ELEPHANTS

THE NIZAM OF HYDERABAD
Pays homage at the Delhi Durbar.

48

Our King and Queen

His Oldest Tenant

In 1909, on one of many visits to his Duchy of Cornwall, he reached Dartmoor in such bad weather that the original plans for the day had to be cancelled. He knew, however, that his oldest tenant thereabouts lived at Whiteworks—she was Mrs. Edwards, aged ninety-two—and decided to call on her. The visit took her aback at first, but, after a quarter of an hour in her parlour, she and her "Duke" were so talkative that they were discussing Mrs. Edwards' reminiscences not only of King Edward but the Prince Consort.

Another time on Dartmoor he was recognised by prison gangs working in the quarries. A convict asked the chief warder if he might call for cheers for the Prince of Wales. It was a foregone conclusion that the request should be refused, but not, one thinks, that it would have been made.

Always Popular

See him and his wife in Lambeth on a visit to the "Old Vic." Thousands of people throng the Waterloo Road and the New Cut. Naphtha lamps flare over stalls laden with food, toys, second-hand tools, cheap clothes, and "nutty stickjaw." A brougham comes along the road. "That's them!" And a roar of cheering carries them across the pavement and into the theatre.

See them in Ireland in 1905—"The country folk had come in from miles around, and the streets of the little town of Cong, usually so quiet and half-deserted, were packed. The cheering was most vigorous" . . . "The district was ablaze last night with bonfires in honour of the royal visit" . . . "Around the station at Dublin a crowd had gathered which heartily cheered the Prince."

This book has nothing to do with politics, but one may be allowed to regret that the constitution barred the possibility of his tackling the whole Irish Home Rule problem as it was revived in the early years of his reign. He intervened quite properly on two occasions, which will be described in their sequence. Each time he provided the only statesmanlike relief to a long tragedy of errors.

Proclamation by the King-Emperor at Delhi

A visit to Germany

His first visit to Germany, as Prince of Wales, was made early in 1902 for the celebration of the Kaiser's birthday. This egregious Emperor, self-styled "All Highest" and "Admiral of the Atlantic," had recently used troops and secret police in an attempt to prevent the letters of his deceased mother, the Empress Frederick, passing out of the country and into the hands of her brother, Edward VII. But the letters had already been smuggled away by Sir Frederick Ponsonby, who had been entrusted with them by the Empress some months before her death at Kronberg, in August 1901.

The Prince of Wales, moreover, arrived in Berlin immediately after a most violent attack by Count von Bülow, in the Reichstag, on Joseph Chamberlain in particular and the British nation in general. He can hardly have relished his journey, nor its object ; but everything passed off successfully. The Kaiser was pleased with the Order of the Garter, his birthday present from King Edward ; and delighted in reviewing his troops. The Prince of Wales contributed to these harmless pleasures by his infallible tact. It may be assumed that he also gained a vivid insight into his Imperial first cousin's increasingly gorgeous mentality.

This mentality envisaged nothing less than a Europe united against the British Empire : It was symptomatic of a sickness best described as "illusions of grandeur." One of these illusions was a contempt for the strength of the Entente Cordiale, which, however, withstood the threat implied by the Kaiser's visit to Morocco—recognition by Great Britain of France's Moroccan protectorate being implicit in the Entente.

The French people, represented most felicitously at the Court of St. James by M. Paul Cambon since 1898, had been entirely converted to friendship with Great Britain by the state visit to Paris of Edward VII in 1903, and President Loubet's visit to London the next year. The Prince and Princess of Wales, who spent a few days in Paris incognito, as Lord and Lady Killarney, in 1908, won all the golden opinions that had been accorded to King Edward. It was

THE IMPERIAL BARGE ON THE GANGES AT BENARES

significant, too, that they won them by their essential Britishness.

The original Entente was extended to embrace Russia, despite the Kaiser's desperate flirtation with the Czar at Bjorke, and in 1907, became the Triple Entente.

Thus the Triple Alliance between Germany, Austria and Italy was offset by the Triple Entente. There was also to be considered the Anglo-Japanese Alliance of 1902. With so much manoeuvring it is no wonder that war became a commonplace of conversation, and that the Germans were toasting "Der Tag !"—or "The Day !"

The Prince of Wales was more in his father's confidence over secret despatches and the general mysteries of govern-

Francis Joseph each wore a military uniform of the other's country ; and to Stuttgart to present the Order of the Garter to the King of Wurtemberg. How pathetic, how futile these memories must have been ten years later.

To India

In 1905 the Prince and Princess of Wales went to India—their real introduction to the rulers and people who were to acclaim them Emperor and Empress at the famous Delhi Durbar of 1911. They took with them a message from King Edward, and their presence, apart from the instant appreciation it roused of their own personal qualities, was of great gratification as an earnest of his good-will.

GARDEN PARTY AT DELHI, 1911

ment than his father had been when Prince of Wales. His naval experience was of great assistance to Edward VII, and his friendship with Lord Fisher, who jolted the Royal Navy into undreamed of activity, placed him among those who contributed to the efficiency of the Grand Fleet in 1914. If anyone thinks that the people were not behind the First Sea Lord and the Prince of Wales in the policy of Insurance against German aggression by sea, let him recall the popular clamour for eight Dreadnoughts in 1909. Mr. McKenna, then at the Admiralty, had asked for six in his programme. The Government thought four would do. The people said : "We want eight, and we won't wait." They got them.

On Tour Again

The Prince of Wales continued his travels with an official visit, in 1904, to Vienna, where he and the aged Emperor

They landed at Bombay, which had come into British possession as part of the dowry of Catherine of Braganza, Queen-Consort of Charles II. It was then as unimportant as Queen Catherine proved to be to her husband. It has developed into a magnificent city with an especially fine natural harbour. King Charles, who never failed in courtesy towards women, must have spent much of his existence as a shade acknowledging to his Queen the great benefit she conferred with her dowry on his country.

The Royal visitors were plunged into a stream of unequalled pomp and pageantry. The homage of rulers, conducted with meticulous regard for imperial ceremonial and the status of each ruler concerned, passed before them in a

AFLOAT WITH HIS NAVY

The King disembarking from a submarine

succession of bejewelled flashes of Indian history. Swords were laid at the Prince's feet: cavalry, still wearing armour, did him clashing honour side by side with a modern camel corps and lancers of the twentieth century: feudal tributes of gold in silken purses were submitted to him to be touched and remitted.

Religious Rites

The Princess was greeted at Bombay with an address from the women—Parsee, Hindu and Mahomedan—of India. Coins and flowers were thrown before her on her way to the Town Hall. The Parsees passed an egg and a coconut, and a bowl of water seven times round her head, on which they afterwards cast rice—all in symbolism of good fortune. The Hindus encircled her with tiny lamps. The Mahomedans garlanded her with flowers and strewed gold and silver about her.

The visit extended from Bombay to Indore, from Indore to Udaipur, to Jaipur, Bikanir, Lahore, Peshawar, the Khyber Pass — where Afridi chiefs brought offerings of sheep and honey — Rawal Pindi — where the military power of the Indian Empire passed by in review— Jammu, Amritsar, Calcutta, Burma, Madras, Benares, Quetta . . .

Here is a glimpse of the Prince bringing down a leaping panther with one shot, and so earning the undying respect of his native beaters: of the Princess in close conversation with the heavily-veiled Begum of Bhopal, India's only woman ruler. Here a performing elephant, tricked out in chain armour, walks about on its hind legs: There men of the Khyber Rifles strain their eyes for stray tribesmen who might be tempted to snipe at the Royal procession through the Pass.

It was a great and marvellous experience for the heir to the throne of the King-Emperor. "We have seen enough to make India a living reality to us," he said, "and enough to make us wish we could see more, and to implant for ever in our hearts sympathy and interest in all that affects our fellow subjects in India of whatever race or creed."

Tragedy in Spain

His next journey was to Spain for the marriage of his cousin, Princess Ena of Battenburg, to King Alfonso on May 31, 1906. It was a wedding day with the associations of a ghastly nightmare. A bomb, in a bouquet of flowers, was flung at the bridal coach on its way from the church; and the Spanish crowds first saw their new Queen as a girl whose

THE QUEEN AND THE PRINCESS ROYAL
Find a joke aboard the Royal Yacht Britannia

pallor only emphasised her self control, her wedding dress bespattered with the blood of a dying soldier, being handed out of the coach by her husband. The Prince and Princess of Wales were in the next carriage, and might well have been struck by bomb fragments.

To Canada

In 1908 the Prince, alone, went to Canada for the Quebec Tercentenary Celebrations, and presided over the final fusing of French and British sentiment. The Plains of Abraham, where Wolfe had conquered the gallant Montcalm and so gained Canada from France, together with the battlefield of Sainte Foy, scene of a British defeat, were purchased by general subscription and dedicated as a national park. Samuel de Champlain, the French founder of Quebec, lived again in a pageant. A review included a detachment of French sailors —who headed the march past— three hundred American sailors, two thousand five hundred of the Royal Navy, and Canadian troops whose appearance evoked the warm admiration of the veteran Lord Roberts.

Naval prestige

The battle-cruiser "Indomitable," with the Prince aboard, made a record for speed on her return voyage to England. She averaged 24.8 knots from Belle Isle to Land's End, consuming 3,000 tons of coal. It was a gesture in which the Royal Navy took great pride, and which was not lost on the Kaiser. The Prince of Wales took a hand in the stoking and emerged from his spell of duty coal-black from head to foot.

Meanwhile the British Government had passed from the Conservatives to the Liberals, supported by the Irish Nationalists and the Labour Party. Sir Henry Campbell-Bannerman, Prime Minister in 1905, was succeeded by Mr. Asquith in 1908. The Old Age Pensions scheme was introduced in 1909, and that same year Mr. Lloyd George's famous "People's Budget" was rejected by the House of Lords with the ultimate result of the Parliament Act which, in the reign of King George, established the House of Commons as supreme in financial matters.

General unrest

There had been unrest in the mines and on the railways. Parties and factions everywhere were getting ready to spring at each other's throats. Old bottles were creaking with new wine. The Suffragette movement initiated a sex-war which, not taken quite seriously by Campbell-Bannerman, showed eventually that women were capable

THE KING ABOARD H.M.S. NEPTUNE

The Duke of York, as a cadet, is on the right

"SHIKAR" LUNCH
IN THE JUNGLE

of embarrassing violence in public as well as private life. Windows were smashed, policemen were assaulted, acid was poured into pillar-boxes, the sacred atmosphere of the House of Commons itself was shattered by screams from the gallery.

Irish politics, too, were becoming explosive. The Nationalists were about to exact from the Liberals the full price of their support.

The Prince of Wales cannot have viewed the antecedents of his accession to the throne with tranquillity. At the same time he never faltered in the preparation for his great office. Politicians may have inspired distrust, uneasiness, and hate. King Edward and his heir remained aloof from popular schisms, while very much in touch with popular feeling and firmly established in popular esteem. It was a joint masterpiece of tact and virile common-sense.

European troubles

Europe, generally, was seething, though the Kaiser had his jack-boot still on the neck of Germany. There were bloody riots in Russia in 1906. King Alexander and Queen Draga of Serbia were hacked to death by military officers in their palace in 1903. King Carlos of Portugal and the Crown Prince were assassinated while driving through Lisbon in 1908. And, in the same year, Austria-Hungary announced that she had formally annexed Bosnia-Herzegovina. That action was to prove fatal to the peace of the whole world.

One event about this time, however, was as fortunate as it was symbolic of that quality of friendly compromise which is the saving grace of the British people. The constitution of the Union of South Africa was signed at Bloemfontein on May 11, 1909. Only the death of Edward VII prevented the Prince of Wales from going out to open the first Union Parliament.

As the reign of Edward VII drew to its close the personality of the Prince of Wales stood out in provocative contrast with those of his two first cousins—the Kaiser, whose mother was King Edward's favourite sister, and the Czar, whose mother was the sister of Queen Alexandra.

The Prince of Wales was the only one of the three who was a man among the people of his country. The others

Tiger Shooting in Nepal

fter the Delhi Durbar

A ROYAL BAG OF TIGERS

THE KING TAKES AIM

59

ANARCHISTS BESIEGED BY TROOPS AND POLICE IN LONDON

The "Sidney Street Siege" of 1911 involved the murder of four policemen by foreign anarchists. They were trapped in a Whitechapel house, and fought back, firing from the windows, until they perished in the flames of the burning building. Mr. Winston Churchill, then Home Secretary, the left of two top-hatted figures, is earnestly watching the activities of Scots Guards and police. The typical Cockney above him is not so serious.

aspired to something a little short of divinity. Poor "Nicky," whose likeness to "Georgie" had so amused Queen Victoria at the Wedding in St. James' Palace in 1893—"it leads to no end of funny mistakes, the one being taken for the other": unhappy man, the "Little Father" of millions who could never bridge the chasm between him and themselves: he was shot in 1919, dying bravely with his wife and children. Nothing can be said of the other, the ex-Kaiser, except that he lives on in shadowy Imperial state at Doorn with his recollections.

But the third, since the death of his father on May 6, 1910, has become more truly a King and an Emperor than the others ever were.

King Edward, though wretchedly ill with bronchitis, insisted on getting up as usual on the day he died. He smoked a cigar. The Prince of Wales brought him news that his horse, Witch of the Air, had won at Kempton Park. The King said smilingly: "I am very glad."

At last they undressed him and put him to bed. Soon after sunset they heard him murmur "I shan't give in! I'm going to fight it!" Coma set in, but he went on fighting until nearly midnight. It was with the birth of the next day that the crowds outside the Palace heard that Edward VII was dead.

George V Succeeds to the Throne

Politics give temporary place to the splendours
of his coronation in Westminster Abbey, and
the Delhi Durbar. He returns from India to
find a nation torn by dissensions.

CHAPTER FOUR

AT the beginning of his reign, King George was in the position of a man who has been riding on the box-seat of a galloping coach-and-four and sees the driver suddenly drop dead by his side. As he takes the reins there is a free-for-all fight going on in the body of the coach, each combatant shrieking advice to him and making it plain that, if he takes other advice, he will be a traitor to the rule of the road.

It was discreditable to all political parties that the King's name should have been used in the bitter hostilities surrounding the Parliament Bill and the Ulster troubles. This was, perhaps, symptomatic of a general hysteria which might well have been infectious to a less balanced, less conscientious monarch. However, if it showed that democracy had lost its head for the time being, the King was proved capable, equally, of keeping his own.

ROYAL VISIT WHICH SEALED THE ENTENTE
The Queen with M. Poincaré, the French President, and the King with Madame Poincaré, in Paris, April 1914.

WAR PROCLAIMED, AUGUST 4, 1914

1914 — 1918

"WE WANT KING GEORGE!" Outside Buckingham Palace after war had been declared

THE KING RIDING TO INSPECT A DIVISION, 1915
LORD KITCHENER IS BEHIND HIM IN THE CENTRE

NEW ZEALAND TROOPS CHEER THE KING AT STEENWERCK, AUGUST, 1916

The King held his first council at St. James' Palace on May 7, 1910, the day after his father's death. He took and signed the oath for the security of the Church of Scotland The Privy Councillors present were re-sworn, and a proclamation of the King's accession was approved. Then the King addressed his Councillors, speaking with evident emotion.

"I am deeply sensible," he concluded, "of the very heavy responsibilities which have fallen upon me. I know that I can rely upon Parliament and upon the people of these islands and of my Dominions beyond the seas for their help in the discharge of these arduous duties, and for their prayers that God will grant me strength and guidance. I am encouraged by the knowledge that I have in my dear wife one who will be a constant helpmate in every endeavour for our people's good."

Note how, for a moment, he substituted "our" for the correct "my" in those last words. There spoke the man, the husband of a perfect partnership. King George and Queen Mary—just as the onlooker may see them when the King formally conducts her into the House of Lords for the opening of Parliament—have always been hand-in-hand.

A ROYAL VISIT TO THE FLEET, 1917

EARTH FOR EVER BRITISH
The King inspecting war graves.

His late Majesty's Privy Council, with numbers of other principal gentlemen of quality, with the Lord Mayor, Aldermen and citizens of London, do now hereby, with one voice and consent of tongue and heart, publish and proclaim—"

The voice rose a note.

"—that the High and Mighty Prince George Frederick Ernest Albert is now, by the death of our late Sovereign of happy memory, become our only lawful and rightful Liege Lord George the Fifth, by the Grace of God, King of the United Kingdom of Great Britain and Ireland, and of the British Dominions beyond the Seas, Defender of the Faith, Emperor of India; to whom we do acknowledge all faith and constant obedience, with all hearty and humble affection, beseeching God, by whom Kings and Queens do reign, to bless the Royal Prince George the Fifth with long and happy years to reign over us."

Then, for the first time concerning the new ruler—"God Save the King!"

Royal proclamation

The proclamation of the King to his people took place the following Monday, on May 9. The first ceremony was in Friary Court, St. James' Palace, and was witnessed by the King and Queen from the windows of Marlborough House.

The crowds were hushed and tense. Over their heads the first fanfare of trumpets winged away into a silent sky. The Duke of Norfolk as Earl Marshal, and Sir Alfred Scott-Gatty as Garter King of Arms, appeared on the terrace over the court. Garter King of Arms, in all the medieval magnificence of his official dress, took a step forward: and one voice spoke in the old way for all.

"Whereas," he said, "it has pleased Almighty God to call to His Mercy our late Sovereign Lord King Edward the Seventh of blessed and glorious memory, by whose decease the Imperial crown of the United Kingdom of Great Britain and Ireland is solely and rightfully come to the High and Mighty Prince George Frederick Ernest Albert: we therefore, the Lords Spiritual and Temporal of this realm, being here assisted with these of

RELICS OF WAR
Re-visiting the Belgian front

THE SMILING SPHINX

Havoc caused by a bomb dropped on the Thames
Embankment, September 4, 1917.

WARNING OF ENEMY AIRCRAFT

TAKE COVER

AIR-RAID DAMAGE IN CROYDON

**CHILD VICTIMS OF THE SILVERTOWN
MUNITIONS FACTORY EXPLOSION, 1917**

TAKING OVER A POSTMAN'S JOB

FIREWOMEN ON PARADE

Women War Workers

PORTERESSES

MISS ENGINE-CLEANER

The hats of the Earl Marshal and Garter King of Arms were in the Air. The people took up the cry with a suddenly released fervour of enthusiasm. Over the garden wall of Marlborough House the King's small sons, on a special platform, could be seen standing rigidly to the salute. Again the clangour of the trumpets. Then, like thunder accompanying this storm of loyalty, the roar of artillery in St. James' Park firing a salute of forty-one guns : and the Royal Standard rose majestically over the roof of Marlborough House.

Other proclamations were made at Charing Cross ; in Fleet Street, just inside the City boundary, and at the Royal Exchange. "Who comes there ?" said the City Marshal, as Bluemantle Pursuivant and his escort approached Temple Bar in the traditional manner : and the reply was— "His Majesty's Officers of Arms who demand entrance into the City of London in order to proclaim His Royal Majesty King George the Fifth."

The Coronation Ceremony
Three million people visited London for the Coronation on June 22, 1911. Contingents of troops from British dominions "beyond the seas" came to honour their King. The country gave itself up to whole-hearted rejoicing : even the hatchet, which had been flashed with such sinister effect over the Parliament Bill, was temporarily buried. The King went to Westminster Abbey as the leader of a people that was united in the symbolism of the coronation.

The Abbey was filled with some six thousand people, of whom only a fraction saw the magnificent and sacred ceremony which invests a British King with the duties and responsibilities of his position. If there were some present who seemed indifferent to the exclusively religious part of the ceremony—and one foreign observer commented on this—the King and Queen were obviously the humblest and most reverent people in the huge assembly.

The Service began with magnificent simplicity. The Archbishop of Canterbury, standing with the King, turned successively to the East, South, West and North, pausing each time to say "Sirs, I here present unto you King George, the undoubted king of this realm ; wherefore, all you who are come this day to do your homage and service, are you willing to do the

The Railway Coach in which the Armistice was signed

THE ARMISTICE WAS SIGNED AT 5 a.m.,
NOVEMBER 11, 1918

ADMIRAL SIR
ROSSLYN WEMYSS

AND

MARSHAL FOCH

who signed the Armistice on behalf of the Allies

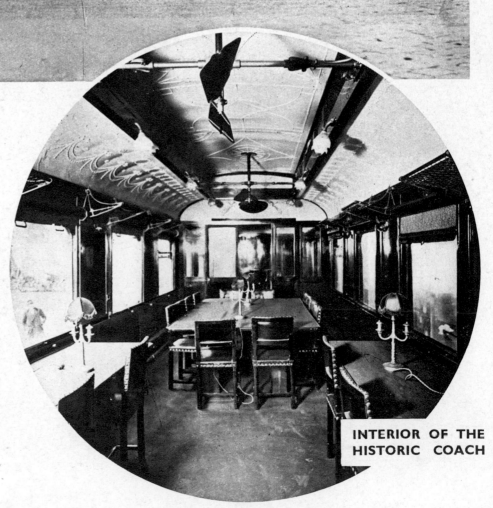

INTERIOR OF THE
HISTORIC COACH

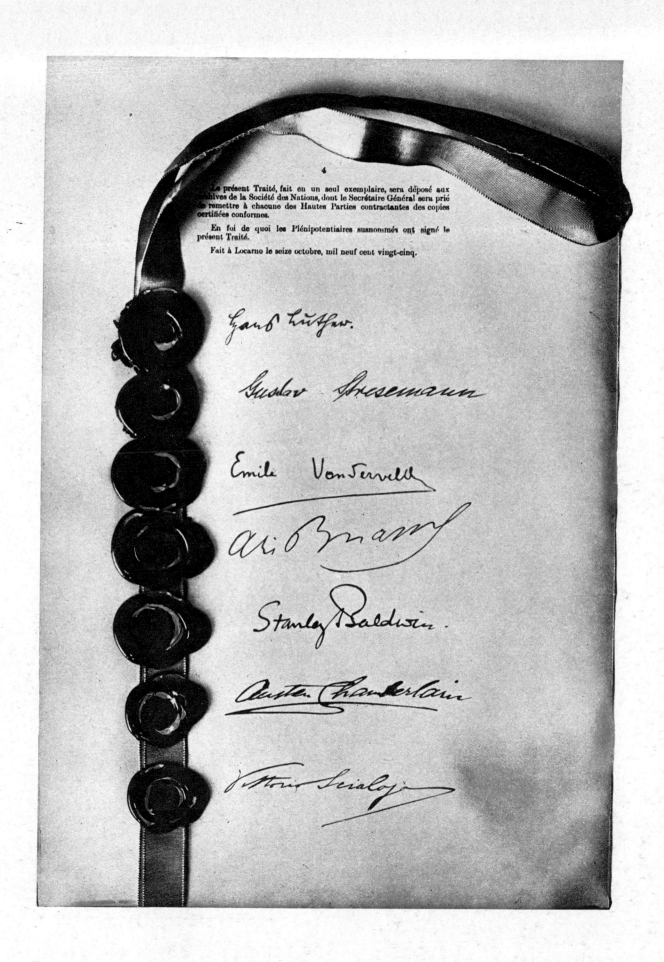

THE LOCARNO TREATY SEALED AND SIGNED IN LONDON
DECEMBER 1, 1925

PEACE PROCLAIMED
IN TRAFALGAR SQUARE

DANCING CELEBRATES THE END OF WAR

CARRYING A LOAD OF HAPPINESS ON ARMISTICE DAY

AMERICAN ADMIRALS AFLOAT WITH THE KING, 1918

Left to right : Earl Beatty, Admiral Rodman (U.S.N.), the King, Admiral Sims (U.S.N.), the Prince of Wales

THE KING AND HIS GENERALS, DECEMBER 19, 1918

Left to right : Sir William Birdwood, Lord Rawlinson, Lord Plumer, the King, Earl Haig, Lord Horne, Lord Byng.

Panorama of the Prince of Wale

Investiture at Caernarvon Castle, 1911

same?" Thereupon the choristers and the boys of Westminster School, representing the people, signified their acceptance of the King with the shout "God Save King George!"—a shout which merged into the splendid voice of massed trumpets.

The supreme moment of the coronation was introduced by the Archbishop of Canterbury asking the King "Sir, is your Majesty willing to take the oath?"

"I am willing," the King replied.

"Will you," asked the Archbishop "solemnly promise and swear to govern the people of this United Kingdom of Great Britain and Ireland, and the dominions thereto belonging, according to the statutes in Parliament agreed on, and the respective laws and customs of the same?"
"I solemnly promise so to do."

"Will you, to your power, cause law and justice, in mercy, to be executed in all your judgments?"

"I will."

"Will you, to the utmost of your power, maintain the laws of God, the true profession of the Gospel, and the Protestant Reformed Religion established by law? And will you maintain and observe inviolably the settlement of the

Church of England and the doctrine, worship, discipline and government thereof as by law established in England? And will you preserve unto the bishops and clergy of England and to the churches there committed to their charge, all such rights and privileges as by law do or shall appertain to them or any of them?"

"All this I promise to do."

The King signed the oath at the altar. Then, sitting in the chair of Edward I, which has been used by all his predecessors, he was annointed on the head, breast and on both hands. Beneath his seat was the Stone of Scone on which Jacob's head is said to have rested when he saw the angels ascending to heaven. Irish and Scottish Kings had been crowned on it for hundreds of years until, in the year 1298, it was captured by the English. Over his head four Knights of the Garter held a canopy of silk and cloth of gold. Consecrated with the holy oil, the King knelt and was blessed by the Archbishop of Canterbury.

He rose and received all the attributes of royalty—ceremonial robes, the sword of state, the sword of justice, the orb, the ring, the sceptre with the cross and the sceptre with the dove; his heels were touched with golden spurs—all the attributes except the crown. The supreme moment had arrived.

A NEW PRINCE FOR WALES

The King presents his son at the King's Gateway, Caernarvon Castle

The crown is a replica of that of Edward the Confessor and was made for the coronation of Charles II. "Oh God," said the Archbishop "the Crown of the faithful, bless, we beseech Thee, and sanctify this Thy servant George, our King, and as Thou dost this day set a crown of pure gold upon his head, so enrich also his royal heart with Thine abundant grace, and crown him with all princely virtues through the King eternal, Jesus Christ our Lord."

As the crown was placed on the King's head a wave seemed to break along the ranks of the peers, who donned their own coronets. The choristers shouted "God Save the King." There was the clash and clamour of great bells : The thunder of guns : A message had gone forth from the Abbey to the people that their king was crowned.

Now he takes his homage. The Archbishop of Canterbury, as Primate of England, is the first to kneel before him. The young Prince of Wales, moving boyishly beneath the immense weight of his robes, takes off his own coronet and sinks to his knees before his father. "I do become," he says, "your liege man of life and limb, and of earthly worship ; and faith and truth I will bear unto you, to live and die, against all manner of folks. So help me God."

The ceremonial is strict ; it provides that the Prince should kiss the King on his left cheek. But all who saw noticed that the King drew his son towards him and returned his kiss.

Now there come to do homage the princes of the Blood Royal and representatives of the peers, who, before they embrace him, touch his crown, as a pledge always to support it with all their power.

After this the Queen is crowned, and with that, all the peeresses place their coronets on their own heads.

The final procession is formed, the Queen going first, wearing her crown and carrying in her right hand the sceptre with the cross and in her left the ivory rod with the dove. Then comes the King, robed in purple. His right hand holds the sceptre, his left the orb. They leave the Abbey and proceed to the Palace. The ceaseless cheering is like the rolling of drums. The National Anthem breaks out spontaneously along the streets. A contingent of overseas troops, dropping discipline, throw their rifles into the air and shout their applause. For two days all is holiday.

The Lighter Side

As a contrast with so much solemnity there are lighter contemporary impressions of happenings about the coronation. Princess Mary, driving with her brothers to the Abbey, is seen waving a threatening finger at the younger ones who affected to be overwhelmed by the robed splendour of herself and the Prince of Wales : and, during the return drive, the Duke of Kent is made to sit on the floor to make more room for his elders and betters. The Duke of Northumberland's two pages while away the long wait in the Abbey annexe by surreptitiously flipping pellets of silver paper—the wrappings of chocolate they had been given to sustain them—at the ranks of immobile guardsmen. And there is the Coronation rehearsal with elderly dignitaries going through their paces carrying swords and insignia made of wood and cardboard.

THE QUEEN
IN COURT DRESS

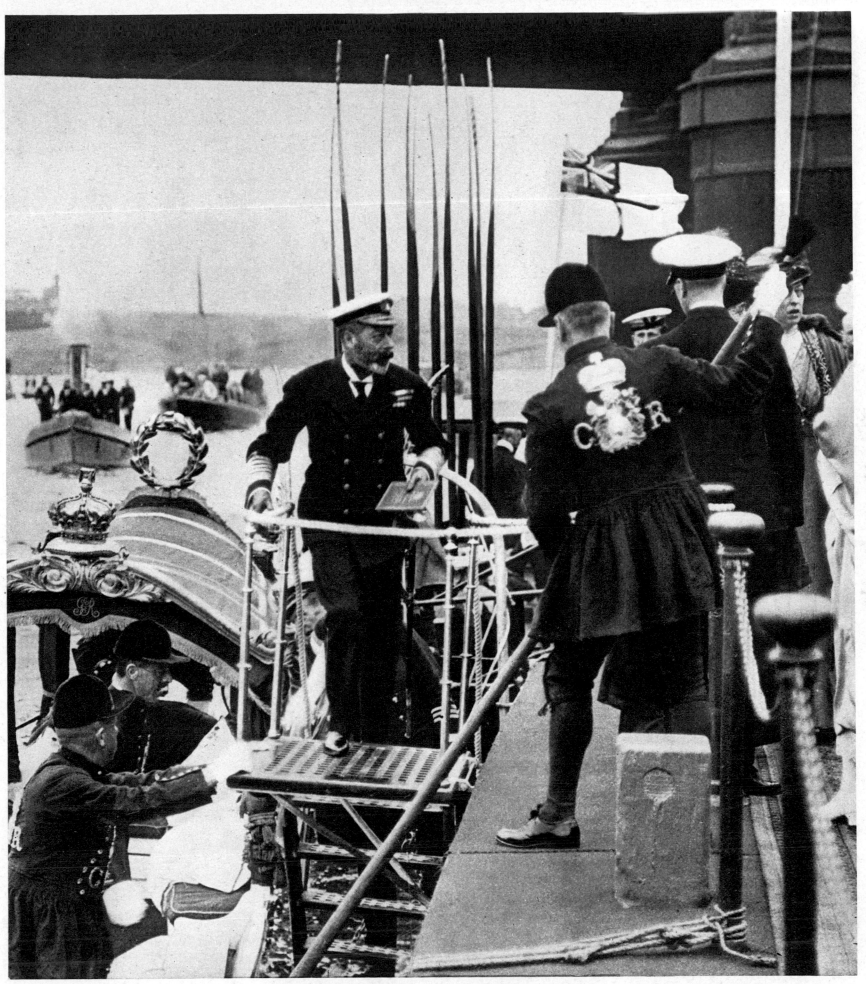

THE KING LANDING AT CADOGAN PIER FROM
THE ROYAL BARGE, THAMES PAGEANT, 1919

77

THE PRINCE BUCKLES A WHEEL
During his visit to Japan in 1922 the Prince of Wales gave Admiral Sir Lionel
Halsey a ride, and was a little too vigorous.

The King had already unveiled the Victoria Memorial on May 16. On July 13 he formally invested his eldest son as Prince of Wales at Caernarvon Castle. Thus the end of one life of duty and the beginning of another were marked with fitting grandeur. There was also marked, with the presence of the Kaiser at the unveiling of his Grandmother's Memorial, the last visit to England of this feverishly-minded emperor.

The pageantry at Caernarvon was a coronation on a minor scale. It was set in blazing sunlight within the grey old castle of which Mr. Lloyd George, as Constable, presented the keys to the King. Everything had been done to honour the Welsh people and their new Prince. The King and Queen sat beneath a canopy with a vacant throne at their side. The Prince was invested with his mantle, his sword, his coronet and his "verge"—a rod of gold signifying his authority. He kneeled again to his father as he had done in Westminster Abbey, but this time he took the oath as "Edward, Prince of Wales;" and as such, he was raised by the King and seated on the throne which was now his. Finally he was presented to the people in the traditional fashion, a slim figure, standing between his father and mother, head of the only principality within the British Empire.

The King's busy year

The remainder of the year was an extremely busy time for the King. He went to Ireland, where the popularity of the royal house was never in doubt. He made a state visit to Edinburgh. He gave a garden party for six thousand people in the grounds of Buckingham Palace and entertained a hundred thousand schoolchildren at the Crystal Palace. He reviewed his fleet, the territorial army, and some thirty thousand boy scouts in Windsor Great Park. As the year was drawing to a close he set sail for India to hold his Imperial Durbar at Delhi, the first King-Emperor of the British Dynasty to appear to his Indian Peoples in their mystic conception of him as the "shadow of God upon earth."

None of the previous emperors had made such a gorgeous progress. None of them had been welcomed with such universal expressions of joy and reverence.

Thousands and thousands made long pilgrimages and suffered great hardships simply to obtain a glimpse of him. The cloths of gold; the priceless jewels; the incredibly rich oriental trappings of state which distinguished the ruling princes, the parades of British and Imperial Service troops—all were welded into a setting for a blaze of the truest imperial dignity. The King-Emperor and Queen-Empress drove to the centre of a vast amphitheatre for their proclamation. Native officers riding behind them carried umbrellas of scarlet and gold, the Indian signs of an emperor's state. There were two pavilions in the midst of this great concourse of troops, and of people who covered ground half a mile long as thick as ants. One pavilion contained the thrones of silver and gold, set on the topmost of a series of marble platforms. Here the King-Emperor and Queen-Empress were proclaimed and here the King-Emperor announced his decision to establish Delhi as the capital of his Indian Empire. In the other pavilion he received the homage of the Viceroy and India's native rulers.

Loyalty

After the troops had left the amphitheatre there was a wonderful and spontaneous surge of the people towards the empty thrones, now guarded by a Highland regiment. Such a demonstration could never take place in this country, but the person of an emperor is regarded with almost religious veneration in the East. The pavilion, so recently occupied by the King-Emperor and his Consort, was besieged by masses who looked upon it as sacred and who strained themselves simply to touch it with their fingers.

Afterwards there was a garden party within the walls of the Fort, and an investiture, at which the Queen appeared as a subject, and kissed her husband's hand on receiving from him the Grand Cross of the Order of the Star of India.

The King returned from India to face an extraordinary succession of political crises. Added to this, the country was torn by industrial unrest, which was envenomed by extremes of passionate feeling. The time had come for him fully to show his qualities both as monarch and man.

THE KING AS COLONEL-IN-CHIEF OF THE GRENADIER GUARDS

EX-SERVICE MEN AND THE KING

Enthusiastic greetings after a review of 20,000 Silver Badge men in Hyde Park

A Nation in Torment

Britain's troubles culminate in the threat of civil war over Ulster. The King summons an Irish conference. Then comes the Great War, and, with it, George V emerges as the true inspiration of his peoples.

CHAPTER FIVE

THE Budget of 1909 seems now such a little thing to have provoked the heaviest artillery of the House of Lords : but it was demolished by them with calamitous results. The electors re-affirmed their confidence in the Government—though the Conservatives won back a hundred seats—and Mr. Asquith proceeded to spike the noble guns which had roared at him so defiantly.

In August, 1911, the Parliament Bill became law. The Lords were deprived of their veto on money bills, certified as such by the Speaker. Any bill passed by the Commons in three successive sessions was to be submitted for the Royal Assent despite the Lords' opposition. The maximum life of a parliament was reduced from seven to five years.

That was the gist of an Act which was glorified as a great triumph for "the people," and which had driven Mr. Lloyd George's detested "dukes" to various apoplexies. In reality it was nothing more than evidence of inability to agree on the reconstitution of a revising chamber which should be at once effective and consistent with the principles of democratic government. Because of that inability the

THE NATION HONOURS EDWARD VII.

Queen Alexandra, between the King and Queen, at the unveiling of the Edward VII memorial statue in Waterloo Place, 1921. The Prince of Wales, in Welsh Guards' uniform, is behind the Queen. The Duke of Connaught and the Duke of York, in Royal Air Force uniform, are behind the King.

The Wedding of Princess Mary to Viscount Lascelles, February 28, 1922

ON THE BALCONY

The King, Princess Mary, Viscount Lascelles (now the Earl of Harewood), Queen Alexandra, and the Queen at Buckingham Palace

CROWDS OUTSIDE THE PALACE, watch husband and wife drive away

ensure its passage. The assurance was published in a letter from Mr. Asquith to Mr. Balfour, leader of the Conservative Party—"in the circumstances, should the necessity arise, the Government will advise the King to exercise his prerogative . . . and his Majesty has been pleased to signify that he will consider it his duty to accept and act on that advice."

As a result, everything was brought into discredit with the "man-in-the-street" except the person of the King.

Mr. Balfour, urged on by the slogan "B.M.G." (Balfour must go), resigned the leadership of the Conservative Party and was succeeded by Mr. Bonar Law, whose virility, especially in the cause of Tariff Reform, did much to disperse the atmosphere of philosophic doubt which Mr. Balfour had spread over his followers. "Pugnacity was wanted and Mr. Bonar Law was chosen."* The Parliamentary Session of 1912 saw the beginning of the agonies of the Home Rule Bill that were to culminate in the fear of civil war. There was also the passage of the National Health Insurance Act to the accompaniment of many protests against slavish "stamp licking," and an assault on Mr. Lloyd George. Payment of members of Parliament had been established. The

* (D. C. Somervell)

THE PRINCESS ROYAL

Colonel-in-Chief of the Royal Scots, presents new colours to the Territorial Battalion of her Regiment.

makeshift, which persists to-day, had to be born of the prostitution to political expediency of the Crown's prerogative of conferring peerages.

This threat had saddened King Edward's last months. It must have been profoundly distasteful to his successor. It was the object of universal satire and derision. How much would the new peers pay for their titles? Mr. Asquith had a list of two hundred and fifty candidates—would there be a reduced price in view of the quantity? And so on.

The Lords were still debating the Parliament Bill when the King put an end to all fireworks by letting it be known that he would create the number of peers necessary to

IN A CHAIR OF STATE

The Princess, at a Girl Guides Rally

THE KING AND QUEEN AT A ROYAL COMMAND VARIETY PERFORMANCE

BRAVERY IN "CIVVIES" LAUGHS WITH THE KING AND QUEEN

Private Samuel Harvey salutes his hosts at a garden party
for three hundred V.C.'s at Buckingham Palace

**THE ROYAL YACHT
"VICTORIA AND ALBERT"**

There was no less fanaticism among the Suffragettes. Windows were smashed, buildings were fired, an explosion was caused in Mr. Lloyd George's unfinished house at Walton Heath ; and, during the Derby of 1913, Miss Emily Davison, worked up by her enthusiasm to the pitch of suicidal ecstasy, threw herself in front of the King's horse, Anmer, and was killed. This shocked all people of both sexes. "The deed she did," runs a contemporary letter to the press "is, of course, open to criticism, to blame, to condemnation. But of her courage, and her sincerity there can be no two opinions, and no single doubt about her devotion to the cause of women."

Never, in all these disturbances, was a gesture made against the King. By all he was recognised, increasingly, as a friend —even if a friend whose actions were circumscribed by constitutional rules.

The suffragettes, who interrupted the Welsh Church was to be disestablished. Electoral reform was promised.

Meanwhile a series of disastrous and especially bitter strikes had begun on the railways and in the mines. The King went to South Wales, where the worst mine trouble had been, and saw conditions for himself. To the consternation of the more short-sighted interests he showed himself an ardent believer in labour conciliation. The Queen accompanied him, and they made a tour of such unaffected sympathy that they won all affection and respect. To take one example—as they were driving through a mining village, a small bunch of flowers and a card was thrown into their carriage. On the card was written "With love from Annie and Mabel."

The Railway Conciliation Boards and the Coal Mines Minimum Wage Act settled the strikes in their respective spheres. Two million workers had been affected. More were to show resentment at their conditions in the London Dock strike, and, in this connection, class hatred was inflamed to fantastic heat. Ben Tillett, addressing fifty thousand people on Tower Hill, prayed that Lord Devonport might be struck dead : and his vast chorus echoed him—"O God, strike Lord Devonport dead !"

THE KING AND QUEEN
Disembarking at Cowes

THE ROYAL YACHT "BRITANNIA" AND HER OWNER

The King, seated just forward of the

wheel, aboard his yacht "Britannia"

THE "BRITANNIA" IN FULL SAIL

progress of a Court in Buckingham Palace by flinging themselves before him and the Queen, and shrieking "Your Majesty, for God's sake, stop torturing women!" well knew that the King had no more hand in the administration of the "Cat-and-Mouse Act" (which provided for the release and re-arrest of hunger striking suffragettes) than he had in the revolutions of the moon. They appealed to him blindly—through him.

Popularity and Friendship

How few kings are capable of real friendship with their people! It says all for the King's character that his attitude has never been considered affected nor condescending. If one lacks a definition of sincerity one has only to watch the King and Queen at a public function, at an "opening," on any of their tours, talking with men and women. Then, to ram the definition home, watch a local personage presiding over a county tea-fight, or "taking the chair in a worthy cause." The contrast is illuminating.

"Good old George—Give us more Beer!"—this, chalked in huge letters along the hull of a ship, once welcomed the King to Clydeside.

"Geordie's all right," said a North of England miner, after

THE KING AT THE WHEEL OF HIS YACHT

THE KING LENDS A HAND ABOARD "BRITANNIA"

one of the King's visits. "He shook hands like a man."

The head of the State and its citizens are at one. His words, a week after his coronation, have proved to be the truth —"Whatever perplexities or difficulties may lie before me and my people, we shall all unite in facing them . . ."

Events abroad

Events abroad were shaping a stormy course. In July 1911, the Panther, a German gunboat, arrived at Agadir, in Morocco, with the avowed intention of protecting the interests of local German subjects. It was the most obvious bluff. The real object of the demonstration was two-fold— to gain some compensation to Germany for France's Moroccan monopoly, and to test further the strength of the Entente. It succeeded in winning recognition of German "influence" over 100,000 square miles of Equatorial Africa, and in inspiring Mr. Lloyd George to speak for Great Britain in explicit terms. "It is essential," he said to a meeting of bankers, "in the higher interests, not merely of this country, but of the world, that Britain should at all hazards maintain her place and prestige among the Great Powers of the world. I would make great sacrifices to preserve peace. But if a situation were to be forced on us in which peace could only be preserved by the surrender of the great and beneficent position Britain has won by centuries of heroism and achievement, by allowing Britain to be treated, when her interests were vitally affected, as if she were of no account in the Cabinet of nations, then I

say emphatically that peace at that price would be a humiliation intolerable for a great country like ours to endure."

That was that : that was the Entente. Germany withdrew for another pounce.

Troubles in Europe

There was war in the Balkans, practically continuously, in 1912 and 1913. Turkey, defeated by Italy in 1911, had Serbia, Greece, Montenegro and Bulgaria at her throat. Then two of the victorious allies, Greece and Serbia, rounded on Bulgaria with the assistance of Rumania. Austria deeply resented the acquisition of so much new territory by Serbia. She almost went to war, but was persuaded by Germany to think better of it. Meanwhile Germany proceeded to increase the peace strength of her army to nearly 900,000 men. There were immediate reverberations, and it was to the tune of them that this country faced dismemberment over the Home Rule Bill.

In Ireland

At this point the King stands out as the one sensible man in his islands. Ulster was arming against her inclusion with the South in Mr. Asquith's scheme of semi-Dominion status for Ireland. The South was arming against Ulster. The Government contemplated the use of the Army as a means of quelling this two-headed revolution, with the result that officers of the cavalry brigade stationed at the Curragh were moved to offer the resignation of their

commissions rather than fight Ulstermen. Someone had blundered again.

The name of the King was again bandied about, in opposition to the Government, as the true object of a soldier's allegiance. Colonel Seely, then Minister for War, suffered the penalty of indiscretion in asserting that the Government would not use military force against the opponents of the Home Rule Bill : and had to resign.

After two gun-running episodes in Ireland—and with bloodshed apparently inevitable—the King attempted to reconcile partisan differences by summoning a conference to Buckingham Palace. If its members had been inspired by a modicum of the royal common-sense, and not so much by self-righteousness, the history of Ireland might well have avoided the Easter rising of 1916 and the subsequent "bad times."

A Noble appeal

"My intervention at this moment may be regarded as a new departure," said the King to his conference of political leaders. "But the exceptional circumstances under which you are brought together justify my action. For months we have watched with deep misgivings the course of events in Ireland. The trend has been surely and steadily towards an appeal to force, and to-day the cry of civil war is on the lips of the most responsible and sober-minded of my people . . . .

"Gentlemen, you represent, in one form or another, the vast majority of my subjects at home. You also have a deep interest in my Dominions overseas, who are scarcely less concerned in a prompt and friendly settlement of this question.

"I regard you, then, in this matter as trustees for the honour and peace of all."

ROYAL SHOOTING PARTY ON THE MOORS

THE PRINCE LEADS THE FIELD

A FATHER'S CONGRATULATIONS
The King shakes hands with the Prince of Wales
after his first point-to-point win in 1921

"JUST AN IDEA" CARRIES THE PRINCE OF WALES WELL OVER A FENCE

95

ROYAL FAMILY GROUP

The King then withdrew, leaving the politicians to their task. Had a nobler appeal ever been made to human feelings? But the Conference, after four days, failed to agree on a solution acceptable to all: and, on September 18, 1914, the King gave his assent to the Home Rule Bill, which, however, was nullified at once by a Suspensory Act. He had acted throughout with perfect propriety. He had been told again and again that he should do this and that. All the irresponsible advice tendered to him, had he taken it, would have caused an immediate explosion on one side or the other. His own advice, which would have made for peace, was neglected.

A man suffering from a violent attack of indigestion is hardly in the mood to give serious attention to external disturbances. Great Britain, in the summer of 1914, with her Irish trouble, gave small thought to Europe. Even Mr. Lloyd George's astuteness seemed at fault when, after the assassination of the Archduke Francis Ferdinand, he assured London bankers that the world's sky was perfectly blue.

Welcomed by the French

In April, the King and Queen had paid a State visit to Paris and received a rapturous welcome. The French admired the Queen's charming sincerity. They found her appearance most queenly and yet with the most delicious appeal. "The King is so thoroughly English," wrote M. Delimal in the Temps, "that, to understand and appreciate him, one must

Smiling in the Rain

THE KING AND QUEEN WITH MR. STEPHEN WALSH
Secretary of State for War, in the first Socialist Government, 1924

97

THE KING BREAKS THE RIBBON
of the new King George V Dock, London, 1921

know something of the British character—know that behind his reserve there are sincere warmth, charming familiarity, loyalty, and fidelity which will stand every trial."* Just those qualities, in fact, which the French were so soon to find in the British Expeditionary Force.

The King and Queen had gone to Berlin, the previous year, for the wedding of the Kaiser's daughter, Princess Victoria Louise, to Prince Ernest Augustus, only surviving son of the Duke of Cumberland. The Kaiser, dazzling in his eagle-helmet, cuirass and white uniform of the Imperial Body-guard, revelled in the attendant military displays. The Czar, almost smothered by precautions against assassination, was a little remote. The King, for whom ordinary police arrangements had sufficed, wore his German uniform of the 1st Dragoons of the Guard with the same simplicity that marked his relations with his two Imperial first-cousins. He stood for peace: the others for force and intrigue. They never met again.

* King George and the Royal Family, by Edward Legge

MR. RAMSAY MACDONALD
after his first interview with the King as Socialist Prime Minister, January 22, 1924. Mr. Thomas, Mr. Henderson and Mr. Clynes are on his left.

In spite of politics the London social "season" of 1914 was exceptionally brilliant, and the weather suited it. Basil Hallam, darling of all light hearts, was singing "I'm Gilbert, the Filbert, the Knut with a Kay!" at the Palace Theatre: and the song suited everyone. Everyone said "He's a knut!" After all, perhaps it was not such a bad world, was it?

The beginning of trouble

On June 28, the Archduke Francis Ferdinand, heir to the imperial throne of Austria, was assassinated at Serajevo, with his morganatic wife, the Duchess of Hohenburg. The police protection for his visit to this hotbed of enmity to Austria was extraordinarily inadequate. There had been a proposal to send special detectives from Budapest, but it was vetoed on the grounds of excessive cost. Almost it seems that Austria wanted her Archduke killed as a pretext for war with Serbia, who could easily be held responsible for instigating the crime. On June 30, von Tschirschky, the German Ambassador in Vienna, informed the German Foreign Office that Austria was spoiling for war with Serbia. His despatch was submitted to the Kaiser, who wrote on its margin "Now or never!"

Austria declared war on Serbia on July 28, and bombarded Belgrade the next day. Europe was mobilising. The assembly of the German High Sea Fleet had been

THE PERMANENT CENOTAPH
unveiled by the King, November 11, 1920

THE KING TAKES A MORNING RIDE WITH HIS SONS

99

The Wedding of the Duke and Duchess of York

THE DUKE AND DUCHESS OF YORK ON THE BALCÓNY
AT BUCKINGHAM PALACE, AFTER THEIR MARRIAGE

THE BRIDE AND BRIDEGROOM
DRIVING ALONG THE MALL

**BRIDESMAIDS AT THE WEDDING OF THE
DUKE AND DUCHESS OF YORK**

countered by a "test mobilisation" of the British Home Fleets at Spithead. Germany declared war on Russia, the champion of Serbia, on August 1, and violated French territory on August 2, declaring war on August 3. That day Albert, King of the Belgians, having rejected the Kaiser's demand for the passage of the German armies across Belgium, appealed to King George. Germany refused to respect Belgian neutrality, and, on August 4, Great Britain declared war on Germany. "Der Tag" had dawned. The witch of war was wedded to military madness, and her dowry was to be seven million dead.

His people always in his thoughts

The King, who had done all he could to preserve peace with his telegrams to the Kaiser and the Czar, came out on the balcony of Buckingham Palace, as the night of August 4 fell, and faced his cheering people. He represented them as he had never done before. He and they were convinced that the nation's cause was just. He embodied now the nation's—the Empire's—determination and hope.

Throughout four years of epic strife and suffering, he

remained a constant example and inspiration, quiet, debarred from sharing the physical agonies of his Forces, behind the facade of the War Cabinet, but always before his people. The demand that was raised during an especially depressed time—"Let the King govern in council!"—only vocalised the respect in which he was held.

Politics at home

A political truce had been declared on the outbreak of war, but a demand for an officially united cabinet resulted in the first Coalition Government which, under Mr. Asquith, lasted from May 1915 to December 1916. It was succeeded by the Second Coalition with Mr. Lloyd George as Prime Minister, and Mr. Bonar Law, leader of the Conservatives, as Chancellor of the Exchequer. This endured until January 1919, and covered the formation of the specialised War Cabinet of five members, who need have no departmental worries, and so approximated to a chairman and directors of the national company.

Memories 1914-18

Many men, even to-day, still have dreams of their war

THE KING MAKES HISTORY IN IRELAND

Driving to open the first Ulster Parliament in Belfast, 1921

t Wembley Exhibition

MAKING FRIENDS
WITH A SMALL PASSENGER

105

AFRICA PROVIDES A ROYAL UMBRELLA AT WEMBLEY

whose appointment to the War Office in 1914 was an inspired act of encouragement, drowned on his way to Russia when the Hampshire was mined ; taxi-cabs, deprived of petrol, running on gas contained in billowing bags on their roofs ; "profiteers" ; the food-shortage, ration-cards, and saccharine pellets instead of sugar ; the Russian revolution and collapse ; the German submarine campaign, and America's entry into the war in 1917 ; air-raids on England ; labour troubles ; conscientious objectors ; women in munition factories, as omnibus conductors, everywhere doing men's jobs ; women as auxiliaries to the Forces—the "Wrens," the "Waacs," the "Wrafs" ; the wounded in hospital "blues" ; man-power running low ; under-nourished war babies ; and the mourners increasing day by day.

Armistice

Finally, the Collapse. The Armistice was signed on November 11, 1918. It was a day of delirious relief. Shops, offices and factories were left to look after themselves. People poured into the streets, shouting and singing. Soldiers were carried shoulder high. Bonfires were lit. Emotions spilled over. Buckingham Palace was besieged again by cheering crowds, half-crazy with joy. They yelled for "good old George !" They sang the National Anthem.

That afternoon the King and Queen, escorted only by four mounted police, drove through London. Abroad with soldiers from all parts of his Empire, afloat with his sailors, at home with his fellow workers, he had never failed in guidance and friendship. That afternoon he and his wife made a triumphal progress, without parallel.

experiences. They live again their parts in a particular raid. The devilish chatter of machine-guns hammers on their pillows. Disjointed memories possess them in weird succession—a comrade's face lit up by a candle-end in a dug-out ; the smell of burning wood under the weeping skies of the Somme ; the whine—rising to a howl—of an approaching heavy shell, and the fountain of mud and filthy smoke into which it exploded ; and those hectic holidays on leave from the battle-front, when one lived, or tried to, at the rate of a day a minute.

While the armies rocked back and forth, the people at home were on the fringe of a nightmare. Everything was feverish —work and play. Again disjointed memories—the introduction of conscription ; the Irish trouble bursting into the Easter rebellion of 1916, and, later in the same year, Lord Kitchener,

TOURING THE EXHIBITION GROUNDS

FATHER AND DAUGHTER-IN-LAW
The King with the Duchess of York at Balmoral. The Duke of York
is behind on the right.

THE QUEEN AND PRINCESS MARY IN A
MILITARY TRACTOR AT ALDERSHOT

Aftermath of the Great War

The Irish settlement. Unemployment increases with industrial unrest. The First Socialist Government and the King. Locarno. The General Strike of 1926.

CHAPTER SIX

THE House of Windsor had been established by Royal Proclamation on July 17, 1917 :—"We, having taken into consideration the Name and Title of Our Royal House and Family, have determined that henceforth Our House and Family shall be styled and known as the House and Family of Windsor . . . and that all the descendants in the male line of Our said Grandmother Queen Victoria who are subjects of these realms, other than female descen-dants who may marry or may have married, shall bear the said Name of Windsor . . . and do hereby further declare and announce that We for Ourselves and for and on behalf of Our descendants and all other descendants of Our said Grandmother Queen Victoria who are subjects of these realms relinquish and enjoin the discontinuance of the use of the Degrees, Styles, Dignities, Titles and Honours of Dukes and Duchesses of Saxony and Princes and Princesses

THE GIPSY'S SALUTE
EPSOM, 1920

THE KING WATCHING TANK MANŒUVRES AT TIDWORTH

WEARING THE BERET OF THE ROYAL TANK CORPS, OF WHICH HE IS COLONEL-IN-CHIEF

of Saxe-Coburg and Gotha, and all other German Degrees, Styles, Dignities, Titles, Honours and Apellations to Us or to them heretofore belonging or appertaining." At the same time enemy Princes who had British titles were deprived of them by Act of Parliament, and all enemy members of British Orders of chivalry were ejected from them. The historians of to-morrow who, in bland repose, may write about yesterday, will find it a little difficult to reconstruct the passions of the War. Yet, however transient the circumstances of the Windsor Proclamation may have been, one excellent result accrued. The British royal house now stands in splendid isolation from its previous Continental entanglements, and with a dignified minimum of "degrees, styles, dignities, titles and honours." Which is precisely as the British people like it.

FOUR GENERATIONS

Alexandra the Queen Mother, with her son, her granddaughter Princess Mary, and her great-grandson the baby Viscount Lascelles.

Letters Patent, dated November 30, 1917, went on to abolish "Highnesses" and "Serene Highnesses," and to restrict the style of "Royal Highness" to the children of the Sovereign, the children of the sons (but not the daughters) of the Sovereign, and the eldest living son of the eldest son of the Prince of Wales. Further, the grandchildren of the sons of the Sovereign in the direct male line—except the eldest grandson of the Prince of Wales—were to have the same title as the children of dukes. Thus, saving the heirs of Royal dukes, there will, one day, be great-grandchildren of the Sovereign known as (say) Lord Albert Windsor and Lady Mary Windsor: and Lord Albert's children will be plain Mr. and Miss Windsor.

VISCOUNT LASCELLES, PRINCESS MARY'S ELDER SON, IS CAPTURED BY HIS BROTHER IN HYDE PARK

OVERLOOKING THE VICTORIA MEMORIAL FROM BUCKINGHAM PALACE
THE WINDOWS GIVE ON TO THE ROYAL BALCONY

112

This rejection, then, of German titles, together with the possibility of the King's descendants becoming commoners, illuminated his position as head, not only of the family of Windsor, but of the British Empire. Four kings—including the Kaiser as King of Prussia—had been deposed in Germany, six reigning Grand Dukes, five Dukes and seven Princes. The Empires of Russia and Austria-Hungary had collapsed. Greece, Turkey, and, later, Spain, also became republics. Each uprising involved the monarchy of the state concerned. All the troubles in post-war Britain were resolved under the monarchy ; and this monarch was so completely dissociated from class feeling as to be the one sheet-anchor of all classes in the storms which blew out of the void of victory.

Bereavement

While the nation was abandoning itself to its joy in peace, still dreaming that victory would produce genuine fruit, the King and Queen were stricken by the death of their youngest child, Prince John, on January 18, 1919. He would have been fourteen the next July. Always delicate, his health had been, for years, a source of anxiety. His parents, his brothers and his sister had loved him with an especial tenderness. At least his end was peaceful. He fell asleep, and, while he was sleeping, the little heart stopped.

* * * *

Anyone, wise after the event, who would condemn the follies of the post-war years in the light of his prejudices, should temper his wisdom to the shorn world of 1919. Nerves were raw : wounds were still bleeding. All councils and conferences, all debates, both public and private, suffered from a general sense of distortion.

Demobilisation released hundreds of thousands of men on the labour market, each of them eager to find the promised land that would be "fit for heroes to live in." A short-lived boom followed the Armistice, much on the principle which governs a dash by school children to a suddenly unlocked tuck-shop ; but it died as peace passed into disillusionment, and strike succeeded strike.

Ireland again

Meanwhile Ireland presented a desperate and murderous problem, with burnings, ambushes, and reprisals in the worst tradition of venomous civil war. Another Home Rule Bill became law in December 1920. It divided Ireland into two self-governing parts. Ulster agreed at once. Sinn Fein did not see its way so clearly. But, while the last scenes of the Irish tragedy were drawn out in the South, the King played a part in the North that was a triumph of personality, and was applauded far outside the theatre of Ulster.

Opening of the first Irish Parliament

He went to Belfast, accompanied by the Queen, and opened the first Parliament of Northern Ireland on June 22, 1921. His decision to do so was, of course, approved by the Government, just as was his speech. The King is the pattern of constitutional propriety. Nevertheless there was a multitude who wanted to believe that he acted and spoke of his own volition, and their very desire emphasised the trust that all his people repose in him. It would be extremely foolish to draw deductions from those well-meaning attempts

CRIPPLED CHILDREN SALUTE THE ROYAL PARTY DRIVING TO ASCOT

"Bad Times" in Ireland

THE FOUR COURTS BOMBARDED, JULY, 1922

BURNING OUT A REBEL STRONGHOLD

THE SIEGE OF THE FOUR COURTS

114

BARRICADES
IN DUBLIN

FORCING AN ENTRANCE

DE VALERA REVIEWS
THE IRISH
REPUBLICAN ARMY

THE QUEEN AT A WELSH PIT-HEAD

to fix this or that responsibility solely on the King: but it surely may be said that never before had so much of the King's self penetrated a speech from the Throne, and never before had his character, as known to his people, been so truly fulfilled as in his appearance in Belfast at the crucial moment in Irish affairs.

The King's Speech

He had a rapturous reception on his way to address the Senators and Members of the House of Commons of Ulster in Belfast City Hall. After he had spoken the whole Empire appreciated his words as those of a great leader. One is always prepared for platitudinous reflections of Governmental policy in the Sovereign's speeches from the Throne. Here, on the contrary, was a King speaking very sincerely and from his deepest convictions.

"This," said the King, to the first Parliament of Northern Ireland, "is a great and critical occasion in the History of the Six Counties, but not for the Six Counties alone, for everything which touches Ireland finds an echo in the remotest parts of the Empire . . ."

"I am emboldened to look beyond the sorrow and the anxiety which have clouded of late my vision of Irish affairs. I speak from a full heart when I pray that my coming to Ireland to-day may prove to be the first step towards an end of strife amongst the people, whatever their race or creed. In that hope I appeal to all Irishmen to pause, to stretch out the hand of forbearance and conciliation, to forgive and to forget, and to join in making for the land which they love a new era of peace, contentment and good-will."

The direct results of his words were the Irish Conference, which at once assembled in London; the "truce," in the South, which was proclaimed on July 11; and the setting-up of the Irish Free State.

The Coalition Government, which had been again returned to power on December 28, 1918, came to an end in October 1922. It had witnessed an almost unbroken series of strikes, and the budding of the tree of "direct action" which was to bear fruit in the General Strike of 1926. It had had to grapple with a housing problem altogether unprecedented. It had swung the "Geddes Axe" of economy in a desperate

ROSE LEAVES FOR A ROYAL BRIDE
Everyone delighted at the wedding of Princess Maud, daughter of the Princess Royal, Duchess of Fife, to Lord Carnegie, son of the Earl of Southesk, 1923

THE BRIDE AND BRIDEGROOM

Princess Maud relinquished her royal title on her marriage

THE KING KISSING THE BRIDE GOODBYE

The General Strike

VOLUNTEER SIGNALMEN

ARMOURED CARS ESCORT
A PETROL CONVOY

VOLUNTEER RAILWAY GUARD

—AND VOLUNTEER OMNIBUS DRIVER

A STEAM-LORRY BRINGS WORKERS TO THE CITY

MILITARY GUARDS FOR FOOD SUPPLIES

THE GREAT MILK DEPOT IN HYDE PARK

VOLUNTEER WORKERS SLEEP ON THE PREMISES

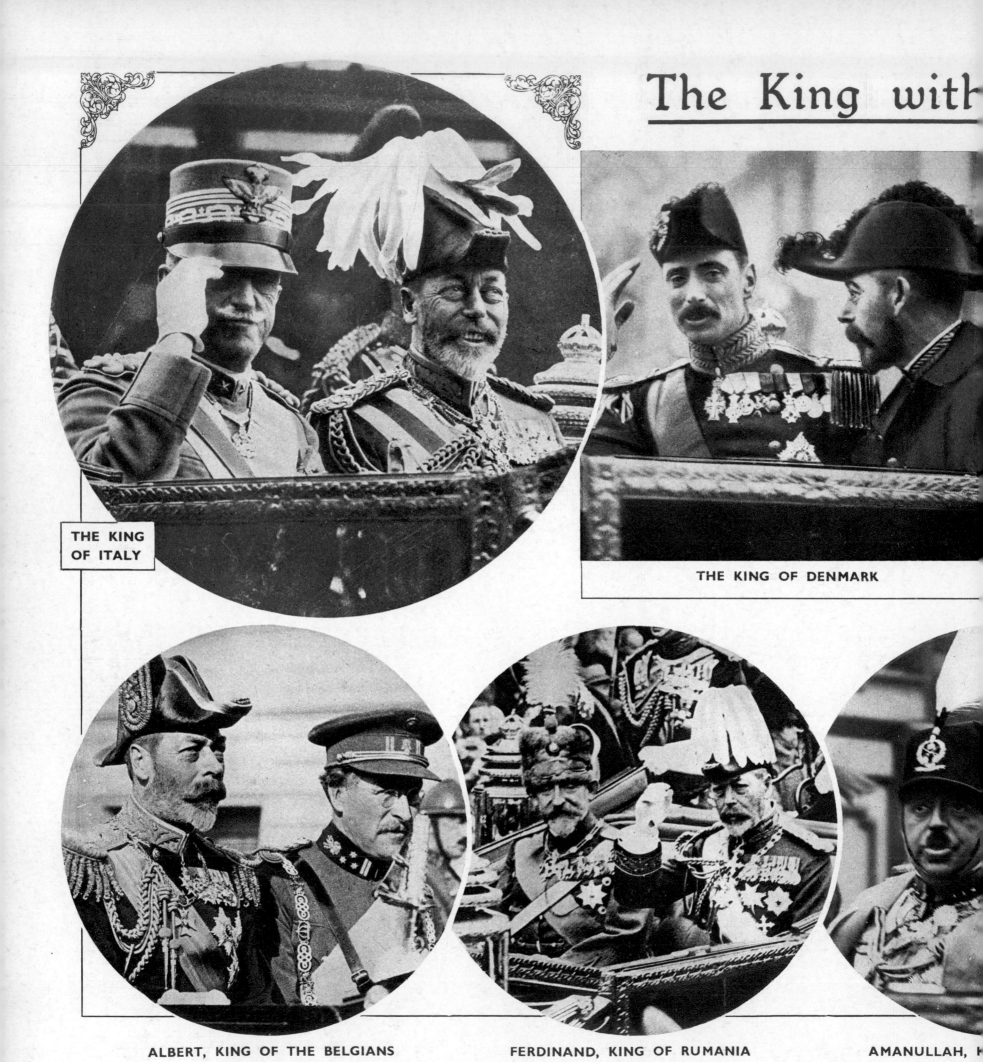

THE KING OF ITALY

THE KING OF DENMARK

ALBERT, KING OF THE BELGIANS

FERDINAND, KING OF RUMANIA

AMANULLAH, K

Foreign Rulers

PRESIDENT POINCARE

KING FEISAL OF IRAQ

AFGHANISTAN

PRESIDENT WILSON

KING FUAD OF EGYPT

BUCKINGHAM PALACE
AND ITS GROUNDS

THE SCENE OF ROYAL GARDEN PARTIES

THE KING AND QUEEN
AMONG THEIR GUESTS

BUCKINGHAM PALACE. THE STATE DINING ROOM
The two glass-panelled doors give access to the Blue Drawing Room and Picture Gallery

THE WEST FRONT OF BUCKINGHAM PALACE
overlooking the lawns and lake

Behind the thrones is the gold-embroidered canopy of crimson velvet, formed from the hangings of the Imperial Shamiana, beneath which the King-Emperor and Queen-Empress took their seats, at the Coronation Durbar in Delhi, 1911.

UP EARLY TO "SNAP" THE KING

CARDINAL MAFFI ESCORTS THE KING IN ITALY

October 30, 1923, he was widely and most sincerely mourned. It is, perhaps, his greatest tribute that his political record has never been assailed by any partisan.

Formation of first Socialist Government

The Anglo-American debt problem was quiescent. A settlement—with whatever unforeseen consequences—had been negotiated by Mr. Baldwin, as Chancellor of the Exchequer. But unemployment was less amenable. Mr. Baldwin, who succeeded Mr. Bonar Law as Prime Minister, was confronted with persistent unemployment figures of well over a million and a quarter. He went to the country, towards the end of the year, on a programme of insular protection and imperial preference—but without food taxes—and was defeated. The Conservative Party was still the largest in the House of Commons, but it was outnumbered by the combination of Liberals and Socialists. Accordingly Mr. Ramsay Macdonald took office, supported by the Liberals, and formed Great Britain's first Socialist government in January, 1924, which was also the year of the first Empire Exhibition at Wembley.

The King was as familiar with the growth of the first as of the second. No other ruler had made himself better acquainted, nor shown greater sympathy, with the people whose Parliamentary representatives followed Mr. Macdonald: and the year 1924 provided no greater foolishness than in the bonnets of old women (of both sexes) who anticipated uneasy relations between the King and his Socialist Ministers.

The Empire Exhibition was the result of his famous "Wake Up, England!" speech in 1901; and had been first mooted at a meeting of the Council of the British Empire League in 1902, which resolved "That it is desirable to hold a British Empire Exhibition as a fitting way of commemorating the memorable journey of the Prince of Wales." The desire, which was realised at Wembley, twenty-two years later, was of the first importance in consolidating Empire interests in peace no less than in war.

New faces—new ideas

The first Socialist Ministers came into office unfamiliar with the traditions of the Court, and—compared with Conservative and Liberal statesmen—unfamiliar with the man who was King. Yet there have been no happier relations between Sovereign and Cabinet than those which existed between the King and the Socialist leaders. It was no foregone conclusion that they should be so, for the King personified a system to which the more extreme members of the Party were hostile and which they openly derided. A little standoffishness and a disinclination to adopt time-honoured formalities was not unthinkable. Those Ministers and the King are in no need of compliments, but the whole nation at the time felt it would like to congratulate—shall one say—itself on the most amiable handling of a new situation.

It was never, perhaps, a reality in the British conception of Socialism that the monarchy should go. There is inherent in the great mass of the people a deep respect and affection for the system of constitutional monarchy. Something in our conception of things must stand firm. The system sets the monarch so far above the wrangles of politics that he stands most securely when parties fall most disastrously.

The Splendour
of the State Coach

THE DUKE OF YORK'S CUP
Tasted by the Queen, after the Royal Navy v Royal Air
Force Polo Match at Ranelagh.

Mr. Tom Griffiths, the first Socialist Treasurer of the Household, had begun life as a half-timer in a Welsh tinplate works. Mr. J. A. Parkinson, the Comptroller of the Household, had been a checkweigher in the mines : Mr. J. E. Davison, the Vice-Chamberlain, successively a bootmaker, foundry-worker and sanitary inspector. "None of us," said Mr. Griffiths, describing their first interview with the King, "felt in the least embarrassed with such a kindly host. It was just as if Labour Ministers were no newcomers to the state rooms of Buckingham Palace. What a delightful half-hour we spent with the King ! He gave me a real good British handshake, and desired that we should talk freely and without restraint. We all made friends at once, and he gave us lucid instructions about our duties, not without a touch of humour."

Thus, four men made a little history that day—freely, without restraint and not without a touch of humour.

Government

The Socialist Government endured until November, 1924. It could not point, any more than the previous administration, to reduced unemployment ; but Mr. Macdonald was able to take credit for initiating a revision of German reparations that led to the Dawes Plan, which was, at least, a palliation of European financial distress. The Government was already wobbling on the shoulders of its restive Liberal support. The hint of a loan to Russia, combined with the mystery surrounding the withdrawal of a prosecution against

—AND THE QUEEN'S CUP OF TEA

IN SPITE OF HIS MAJESTY HAVING PASSED A FAIR NIGHT, THERE HAS BEEN A SLIGHT RISE IN THE TEMPERATURE SINCE YESTERDAY. THE GENERAL CONDITION REMAINS UNCHANGED.

(SIGNED) STANLEY HEWETT
DAWSON OF PENN.

10.30 A.M.
1ST DECEMBER. 1928.

BULLETINS OF THE KING'S PROGRESS
were fixed to the Palace railings

CROWDS OUTSIDE BUCKINGHAM PALACE DURING THE KING'S ILLNESS, 1928

Convalescence

HIS FIRST PUBLIC APPEARANCE
Bognor, April, 1929

Mr. J. R. Campbell, a Communist editor, whose publication urged soldiers to mutiny rather than fire on strikers, was sufficient to bring it down. The "Zinoviev letter," which incited British Communists to revolution, was thrown in during the election. There was a swing over to Conservatism, and Mr. Baldwin again found himself Prime Minister with an absolute majority. In this position he remained, more or less tranquilly, until June 1929—a period which embraced the Locarno Treaty and the General Strike.

The King had become a grandfather on February 7, 1923, when a son was born to Princess Mary, who had married Viscount Lascelles, now the Earl of Harewood, on February 28, 1922. In the same year—April—his second son, the Duke of York, had married Lady Elizabeth Bowes-Lyon, youngest daughter of the Earl of Strathmore and Kinghorne. The match was especially popular because of the bride's nationality and her non-royal status : it became a matter of enthusiastic applause when people saw her, and came under the spell of her personality. Her smile, it had always been said by her friends, made one love her : and the crowds wholeheartedly agreed. Both her daughters have inherited it.

A Grandson, and Daughter-in-law for the King

Moving among his people during these years, visiting industrial areas, performing innumerable opening cere- monies—of which the most impressive was in the vast

IN THE GROUNDS OF CRAIGWELL HOUSE

The King Returns to Health

and his people, 1929

THE PRINCE OF WALES
AND HIS AIRPLANE

covers thirty-three of the thirty-five millions of world telephone subscribers. Japan was added on March 12, 1935, and communication with Shanghai, Kenya and Iceland was established during the Jubilee year.

Bereavement

To the great grief of the King and his family, Alexandra, the Queen-Mother, died on November 20, 1925, aged eighty-one, following a heart attack six days before. No lovelier princess had ever come to England ; no gentler, more Christian spirit had ever animated womanly beauty. She gave most of her income to charity. Every day since his boyhood the King had read a chapter of the Bible at her request : and, every day, he either saw her or wrote to her. Her funeral procession passed through London to the wail and crash of mourning music, while snow fell softly over her in whose nature had reigned eternal summer.

THE DUKE OF YORK
AT A CAMP
FOR SCHOOLBOYS

Anglican Cathedral at Liverpool—at sports and race-meetings, at Court and in the country, the King was no gracious figure-head, but a shrewd, knowledgable man forever anxious to extend his already enormous experience. "I am tremendously impressed," said Mr. R. C. Morrison, Socialist Member for North Tottenham, speaking to his constituents in 1924, "by the King's up-to-date information of what is going on." He was also delightedly impressed with the King's sense of humour. Mr. Morrison had remarked that he would have borrowed a fireman's helmet from the Tottenham Brigade, if he had known what gorgeous array prevailed at the Speaker's levee. Later, he was present at a Court function. "Well, Mr. Morrison," said the King, smiling, "have you brought your fireman's helmet?"

Christmas Broadcasts

Broadcasting made it possible for the King to enter the homes of millions who might never see him, particularly in his overseas Dominions. His voice was heard on the air for the first time in April 1924, at the opening of the Wembley Exhibition. But his Christmas broadcasts, beginning in 1932, have proved not only the most dramatic but by far the most moving of these miraculous contacts. Their influence for unity and good-feeling has been incalculable. His voice, resonant, sincere, paternal in the happiest sense, has inspired genuine affection among men, women and children thousands of miles away.

The public foreign telephone service has been greatly extended, with the aid of radio, since the time of the War, when Great Britain could speak only with France and Belgium. Now it

THE DUKE OF GLOUCESTER SHIES AT COCONUTS

The King had suffered an attack of influenza in the spring of 1925, which necessitated a Mediterranean cruise. He landed in Italy, where he had paid a State Visit two years before, combined with a tour of war-graves.

The Locarno Treaty

In 1925, a variety of pacific junketings abroad by European statesmen culminated in the signing of the Locarno Treaty, which may be compared with the use of a deodorising spray in an old-fashioned, stuffy cinema. The effect was temporarily refreshing, but the stuffiness returned with double force. There had been much oratory of the blooming kind. When the blossoms withered it became apparent that Great Britain was hopelessly committed to the probability of European hostilities. The return to the gold-standard on April 29, 1925, was another gesture which, hailed as beneficent by the majority, proved profitless. It was a boomerang gesture of pride, for our exports soon declined. The gold-standard was again abandoned on September 21, 1931.

Lord Balfour's definition of the Dominions' status, at the Imperial Conference of 1926, was one of the more fortunate events of this time. It allayed various irritations—such as Canada's resentment

THE DUKE OF KENT

takes a run in South Africa

135

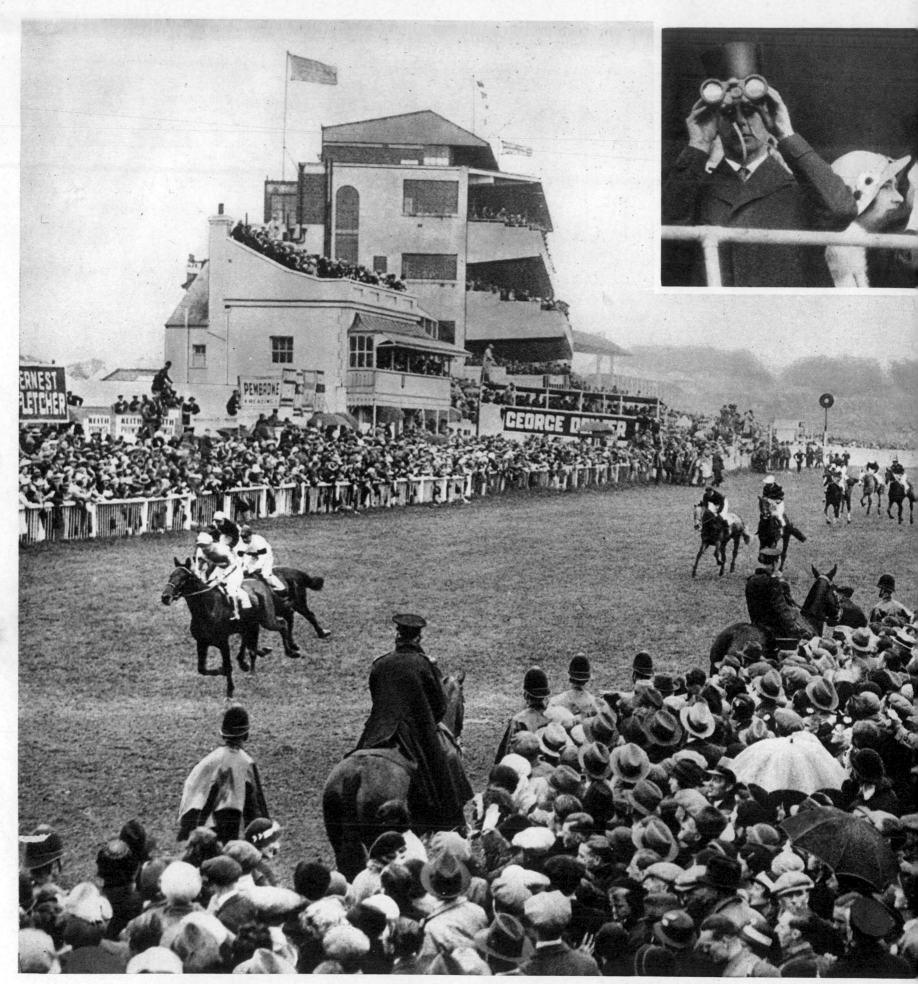

All Eyes on the Field : the Royal Famil

THE PRINCE OF WALES WITH "OLD KATE"

RACING HAS ITS HUMOURS

t the Derby of 1934

THE ROYAL BOX
AT ASCOT

at being called on to supply forces during the Chanak crisis—and strengthened all the links of Empire. Great Britain and the Dominions were recognised as "equal in status, in no way subordinate one to another in any respect of their domestic or external affairs, though united by a common allegiance to the Crown, and freely associated as members of the British Commonwealth of Nations."

The General Strike

The summer of 1926, was blackened by the General Strike, which proved to be a trial of strength between the militants of Trade Unionism and the State, never likely to be repeated. What chiefly emerged was the people's decision that national security came before party disputes ; and, however much sympathy the miners deserved in the terrible depression of their industry, that nothing justified a potential revolution. The Strike lasted from May 4 to May 12 : all vital industries and services were involved : but the emergency measures taken by the Government, with

DRIVING UP THE
COURSE

PRINCESS ELIZABETH AND PRINCESS MARGARET PULL THEIR WEIGHT

no lack of volunteers, maintained national life and food-supplies practically unaffected. In the end the strike was called off for the resumption of negotiations. There had been no barricades, no shootings—inevitable consequences of a similar upheaval in European countries—and the country could be thankful with reason for its basic British good sense.

A human episode

There was a very pleasant incident in the King's life towards the end of that year : and one which had wider publicity in America than in this country. He bought a half-share in a rabbit.

THE KING'S GRAND-DAUGHTERS

The Princesses Elizabeth and Margaret

Posing for Father

A pretty picture of Princess Elizabeth, taken by the Duke of York

Little Kathleen Tomlinson, daughter of the Rev. C. F. Tomlinson, Rector of Bolton Abbey, met the King while he was there for the shooting. She had a pet rabbit, a great joy to her in convalescence from an illness, and introduced it to the King, telling him, at the same time, that she was about to lose it because her brother had promised his share in it to someone in the village.

The King said he thought this was rather a shame ; and a few days later, Sir Charles Cust, the King's Equerry, approached young Master Tomlinson with an offer to buy his half-share on behalf of the King. There seem to have been complications attached to the transaction, but, eventually, it was settled that Sir Charles would give ten shillings for the boy's share—"Then," he said, "the King will have your half-share, and will give it to Kathleen. She will have all the rabbit and you will have the ten shillings."

An American point of view

There was an interesting American comment on this happy affair—"No such thing," said a leader-writer in the World, "could happen in this country. If an American President were to try it, even if he acted from the simplest motives, the smell of the press agent would hang about the story, but no such smell hangs round this story. The King of England needs no press agent. He does not come up for re-election. He never lacks for fame. He is born famous and he can never lose his job. Even if he ceases to rule he is still a King. In this instance the King merely exercised the one great privilege of a King—to be a simple human being."

The King's Illness of 1928

Equal Franchise and Women's Freedom. The
Second Socialist Government. Snowden electrifies
Europe at the Hague Reparations Conference.
New Movements.

CHAPTER SEVEN

WHEN the King opened Parliament on November 6, 1928, it was evident that the prevalent cold had slightly affected his voice.

The Prince of Wales was away, hunting in East Africa, with the Duke of Gloucester : so his gilt chair, which is immediately to the King's right, only a step lower than the royal thrones, was empty. Otherwise the beautiful ceremonial remained the same as always.

The galleries are crowded with guests more or less distinguished, among them the Lord Mayor of London who, within the boundaries of the City, owns no superior but the King. The Commons, headed by Mr. Speaker, are at the Bar of the House of Lords. Ambassadors form a splendid mosaic of uniforms and decorations. There is a rustle of talk and laughter until the blaze of lights hanging from the roof is dimmed to a cluster of glow-worms. This signals the approach of the royal procession. Now there is a hush, and the light under the canopy over the thrones burns alone.

From the door on the right of the dais—as one looks up the House—there enter those survivors of ancient chivalry, the officers of the College of Heralds. They wear uniforms like the dress of Court cards. As they are grouping themselves, all the lights blaze again, the House rises, and, from the opposite door, come the Lord Chancellor, the Usher of the Black Rod, the Earl Marshal, the Lord Great Chamberlain, the Sword of State carried by a Peer, the Cap

PRINCESS ELIZABETH DRIVING WITH THE QUEEN AND HER MOTHER FROM THE CEREMONY OF TROOPING THE COLOUR

THIS IS GOING TO BE A GREAT PARTY— for two small **Princesses** at the **Braemar Gathering**.

of maintenance—crimson velvet and ermine—carried by a Peer, and, finally, "The King's Most excellent Majesty," accompanied by the Queen.

Their trains are carried by pages. They wear their crowns. A legend comes true with their entrance, hand-in-hand.

They walk to the centre of the floor and bow to the assembly. Peers, bishops, ambassadors, and peeresses bow low in return. The King hands the Queen up the steps to the throne, and they take their seats. Their trains are draped on either side by the careful pages. The Sword of State and the Cap of Maintenance flank the dais. The Mistress of the Robes and the Queen's Ladies stand beside her. "My lords," says the King, "pray be seated."

The Lord Chancellor advances, bends a knee, and hands the King the copy of his speech. The Crown flashes as the King inclines his head and begins to read—"My Lords and members of the House of Commons . . ."

November 11th

Five days later, the King attended the Armistice Day Service at the Cenotaph. It was a raw, chilly day, misty, with slight rain. The Two Minutes' Silence was sodden and oppressive : suddenly, tearingly, a woman

began to cry at the weight of it : the first decade of mourning was completed and the dead were leaning hard against the memories of the living. Ten years ! Never again can it be quite like that.

Beginning of a long illness

After a short visit to Sandringham the King returned to London in poor health, and, on November 21, a bulletin signed by Sir Stanley Hewett and Lord Dawson of Penn, was issued from Buckingham Palace stating that "His Majesty the King is suffering from a cold with some fever, and is remaining in bed." This was the first news to the public of an illness which was to develop so as to tax the patient's reserves to the utmost, and from which he did not completely recover until the following Summer. The expression of public concern was profoundly affectionate, and spread from London throughout the Empire.

The Prince of Wales, who had telegraphed from Tanganyika on November 28, that he was returning at once, arrived in London on December 11, and saw his father that evening. "I believe it is quite true," recorded the late Lord Brentford (then Sir William Joynson-Hicks), "that when the Prince first went in to see his father, not knowing whether he would be conscious or unconscious, the

PENGUINS ON PARADE FOR THE KING

In the Edinburgh Zoological Gardens

143

THE WEDDING OF THE DUKE AND DUCHESS OF KENT IN WESTMINSTER ABBEY, NOVEMBER 29, 1934

King's first words were : "Well, David, did you get that Lion ?"*

A week before there had been official announcement of the Commission appointing the Queen, the Prince of Wales, the Duke of York, the Archbishop of Canterbury, the Lord Chancellor, and the Prime Minister "Counsellors of State" to act, generally, on the King's behalf. It began—"Whereas we have been stricken by illness and are unable for the time being to give due attention to the affairs of Our Realm . . ." and was addressed to "all Archbishops, Dukes, Marquesses, Earls, Viscounts, Bishops, Barons, Baronets, Knights, Citizens and Burgesses and all others Our Faithful Subjects whatsoever."

Sympathy of a Nation

That was read in its formality and forgotten by the people. But they will remember "Jix's" story for a long time—the King and his Counsellor, the Prince of Wales ; the sick father and his son ; "Well, David . . ." Thus the family concept of monarchy is suddenly illuminated and is translated, in popular terms, to countless family firesides. And it is because the present holder of the British monarchy is just so cherished that "Old Kate," who had often sold him a race-card on Derby Day, clung wet-eyed to the railings of Buckingham Palace during his illness.

The King returned in health to London on July 1. He and the Queen had motored from Windsor to Kensington. There they entered the first of three open carriages, and so, by way of Knightsbridge, Piccadilly, St. James' Street, and the Mall, began a homecoming that showed, as had no other popular demonstration, the love of his people. For this occasion was concerned with no war, with no international policy : it was purely domestic, a family party of the happiest kind to celebrate the return of the head of the family from a long, arduous journey. From the Albert

* "Jix," Viscount Brentford, by H. A. Taylor

"BE CAREFUL !"

Princess Margaret lifted up by the King to see the crowds outside the Palace, on the Duke of Kent's wedding day.

Hall to Buckingham Palace cheers swept him along. In Piccadilly, leaning over a balcony in the Duke of York's house, a little girl frantically waved a flag at her grandfather, and the King laughed back at Princess Elizabeth, who had been his most delightful visitor at Bognor Regis. Finally, thousands in front of the Palace sang the National Anthem, and shouted again and again as the King and Queen bowed their gratitude from the balcony.

The Thanksgiving Service which followed in Westminster Abbey symbolised a sentiment that was common to all creeds and sects within the Empire.

The new times produced new figures. Colonel Lindbergh made a record non-stop solo flight from New York to Paris on May 20 and 21, 1927—a worthy successor to the first West to East transatlantic flight by Sir John Alcock and Sir A. Whitten Brown from Newfoundland to Ireland, in June 1919, in a wartime nightbomber.

BRIDE AND BRIDEGROOM
The Duke and Duchess of Kent

Britain Leads the World

NEW LAMBETH BRIDGE, LONDON
opened by the King, 1932

WORLD'S LARGEST LINER, "QUEEN MARY," launched by the Queen, on the Clyde, 1934.

THE LARGEST DRY DOCK in the world opened at Southampton by the Royal Yacht, Victoria and Albert, 1933.

WORLD'S GREATEST SINGLE SPAN BRIDGE over Sydney Harbour, opened for traffic, 1932

WORLD'S LONGEST TRAFFIC TUNNEL under the Mersey, opened by the King, 1934.

AUSTRALIA'S NEW COMMONWEALTH PARLIAMENT BUILDING
OPENED BY THE DUKE OF YORK, IN CANBERRA, MAY, 1927

THE DUKE OF GLOUCESTER INVESTED BY KING NEPTUNE

with the Order of the Grand Pacific, crossing the "line"
homeward bound from his Australasian Tour, 1935

King Amanullah of Afghanistan, flying all too rapidly for his subjects towards Western ideals, arrived in England in March, 1928, and had a glorious period of sight-seeing. He returned to his restive realm suffering from a surfeit of European civilisation, and with the most unfortunate results. Afghanistan, unprepared for his sweeping reforms was badgered from bewilderment into rebellion.

The signing of the Kellogg Pact " to outlaw war" was a meaningless if beautiful gesture of 1928. Its only peaceful consequence on which one could put a material finger was the awarding of the Nobel Peace Prize to its begetter, Mr. Kellogg, the American statesman. In the same year the New Prayer Book was finally rejected by the House of Commons. The effect of this vote, hostile to the reservation of the sacrament, was precisely nothing. Those who had practised reservation continued to do so, but with the knowledge that their practices were now illegal.

World-Wide Knowledge.

There can have been few of the King's subjects who were harder worked in this post-war decade than the Prince of Wales. He was serving an apprenticeship just as his father had done, and, in the series of tours which he made, his father's guiding hand may be well imagined. The King, far ahead of many of his contemporaries, had thought never in terms of the British Isles but the British Empire. The Prince, as with the whole royal family, has the same mind. Anyone can discuss the Empire in fluent, persuasive phrases ; but the Prince has actually visited most parts of it, with the result, so disconcerting to professional wind-bags, that when he gets on his feet to speak, say, of the fruit-canning industries of Victoria, he does know what he is talking about.

He brought back with him the same attitude towards home apathy that the King had evinced in his "Wake Up, England !" speech. It was not enough, he found, to make the goods for sale abroad : the goods must be sold against the wiliest competitors : and in salesmanship the British are only too apt to sit back and wait for orders.

Royal Annoyance.

On the other hand there are, sometimes, apparently immovable obstacles in the salesman's path, and it was one of these that annoyed the King on a famous occasion. He was looking at British-made typewriters at the British Industries Fair, and was told that the Swedish Government had ordered a large consignment of them. "But," proceeded the sales manager, " the typewriters used in our own Government departments are foreign makes."

THE QUEEN AS DOCTOR OF LAWS OF ABERDEEN UNIVERSITY

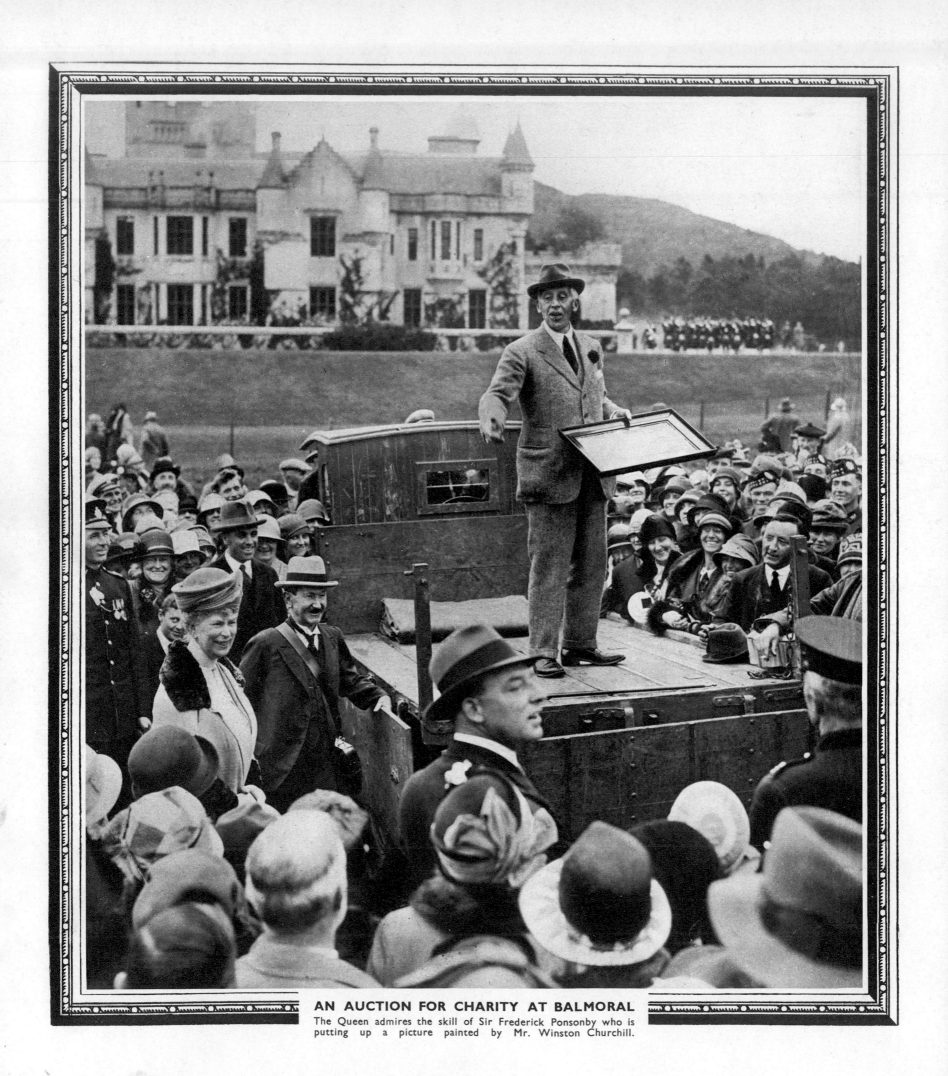

AN AUCTION FOR CHARITY AT BALMORAL
The Queen admires the skill of Sir Frederick Ponsonby who is putting up a picture painted by Mr. Winston Churchill.

A GOOSE MAY LOOK AT A KING
or so thinks this pet of a Cavalry Regiment.

IN MEMORY OF GUY FAWKES

Yeomen of the Guard arriving to search the Houses of Parliament.

The King Opens

His arrival at the House of Lords, and hi

152

PEERESSES LEAVING THE HOUSE OF LORDS.

Parliament in State

ogress across the Horse Guards Parade.

A RING OF ROSEBUDS ROUND THE QUEEN

"This is scandalous," the King was reported as saying, "scandalous. If other Governments can purchase these machines, why cannot they be used in our own departments? I will have the matter looked into." It was just the sort of royal remark it does an ordinary man good to hear.

Results of "Votes for Flappers".

Meanwhile Mr. Baldwin's Conservative Administration, after a gloomy flirtation with the reform of the House of Lords, and a spectacular raid on "Arcos", the Russian Trade Agency in London, in search of Bolshevist propaganda, had extended the franchise to women equally with men, and so faced a general election in the Summer of 1929.

The most appalling consequences were prophesied of the so-called "Flappers' Vote": and, when the Conservative strength fell from 396 members to 260, while the Socialist increased from 160 to 290 and the Liberal from 46 to 60,

there were bitter wails to Mr. Baldwin of "I told you so." It is now considered, however, from the distance which lends enchantment, that the new women electors were not of themselves responsible for the swing-over, but simply increased the already determined proportions of votes. In any case the same electorate was glutinously congratulated by the wailers of 1929 when it made National Government possible two years later.

A Strange point of view.

The Equal Franchise Act was the merest justice to women. They had had the vote at the age of thirty for ten years, and it was intolerable that they should continue to be regarded as stupider at twenty-one years than the average male of the same age. More, it was incredible. Especially as a woman of twenty-one had been able to stand for Parliament while not allowed to vote for a candidate all those years. In other words, she had been considered fit to legislate but not fit to vote for legislators.

STEEL, CONCRETE AND GLASS, MAKE MODERN BUILDINGS

The Daily Express building, Fleet Street, London.

the seductive tune of the "Blue Danube" which our mothers had never thought to hear again, but which typified the rebellion against rhythm divorced from melody and the reign of "jazz".

Self Sacrifice.

Fascism in Italy, and its counterparts in Germany and Austria, betokened a revulsion from Communism ; but this country has been wooed effectively by neither side. Its patriotism remains the least aggressive, the least politically minded in the world.

One concomitant of Italian Fascism, on which there must be universal congratulation, was the Vatican Treaty of February 11th, 1929, which healed the breach between the Pope and Italy, and recognised the complete sovereignty of the Holy See in the Vatican City. All claims against the State for loss of temporal power were finally settled, and the Sovereign-Pontiff left the Vatican, in which all Popes since 1870 had voluntarily confined themselves as a protest, for the first time on July 25th.

To return to home affairs, the report of the Economy Committee had appalled the country and split the Socialist Cabinet. Cuts in expenditure and salaries were everywhere imperative, but it seemed especially tragic that a cut should be necessary in the unemployment benefit. Ultimately Mr. Macdonald, with Mr. Snowden, Mr. Thomas and Lord Sankey, the Lord Chancellor, found themselves opposed to Mr. Henderson and the rest over proposals to effect economies and to balance the Budget.

films, to tales of "good old days" and "better times" ; and also a dwelling on filth for filth's sake as if to harden oneself to any assaults.

The post-war decade also saw the growth of road-houses consequent on the vastly increased number of motorists. The cult of fresh air and sunshine bred clubs of "hikers," and colonies of "nudists". Women's skirts crept up above their knees in obedience to the ugliest fashion yet decreed for the sex, were obviated to some extent by an epidemic of "Russian boots", and crept down again to

If Mr. Macdonald had the support of the Opposition, he had the violent hostility of the Trade Union Council. He had also the knowledge that he must live up to his election-standard in some way and do something. It was a deplorable dilemma, with erstwhile colleagues turning into enemies under the lash of circumstance.

At this point, when the prospect seemed blackest, the King, who was in Scotland, left Balmoral for London. The one man who could save the situation had appeared, not only in accordance with his duty, but to the inexpressible relief of the nation.

The King and the Crisis

CONCLUSION

THE national necessity in August, 1931, was threefold. The Budget had to be balanced : credit had to be restored : confidence had to be re-established in political Providence. It seems almost a truism now to say that this semi-miracle could not have been performed by any one of the three parties appealing alone to the electorate in the face of the prevalent confusion and distress. The nation required a psychological tonic, and a suggestion of union was the handiest dose.

Mr. Snowden had already said : "We can return to party bickering later." It was now imperative that bickering should stop.

The King, who had been in the closest touch with events on the information of his Prime Minister, decided to leave Balmoral on Saturday, August 22. As he rushed London-wards, Mr. Macdonald's cabinet was in the last throes of an earthquake. It collapsed in wreckage on Sunday, and, that evening, the Prime Minister visited the King at Buckingham Palace with his hopeless news.

It has been said before that the King is the model of constitutional propriety. To credit him with the formation of the National Government would be as great an insult as to blame him for any of its subsequent faults. What the King did, in pursuit of his recognised triple right to be consulted, to warn, and to encourage, was to exercise his principal constitutional function which is "to supply the nation and the Empire with a rallying point, and a unifying principle, entirely above party."[*]

The following morning, Mr. Macdonald, who had adopted the King's suggestion to sleep on his difficulties, returned, bringing with him Mr. Baldwin and Sir Herbert Samuel as leaders of the Conservative and Liberal Parties. There was a brief but very frank discussion with the King, who then left the three statesmen to hammer out an agreement which could be submitted to him by the Prime Minister.

Soon after four o'clock that Monday afternoon Mr. Macdonald saw the King again and tendered the resignation of the Socialist Ministry. He was thereupon commissioned

[*]The Constitutional Year Book

EGYPTIAN MOUNTED POLICE
VISIT BUCKINGHAM PALACE

The First King to Broadcast to his People all over the world

official visitors. In the middle of the day he usually takes a walk in the Palace gardens. Then there is more work until tea, the meal which is said to be his favourite if he is free to have it in the Palace, and over which he can sit and talk with the Queen, the business of Kingship momentarily forgotten. Afterwards there may be more official visitors. And there are frequent public engagements.

Pastimes

Yachting and shooting are, perhaps, his best-liked recreations. His collection of stamps—world-famous and extraordinarily valuable—is the hobby to which he devotes much of the time he can spare. He has also a wonderful collection of antique clocks and watches. His pets have long included an elderly grey parrot called "Charlotte," and he has now a great friend in his Cairn terrier "Bob" who succeeded the lamented "Snip," his companion for seven years.

Mannerisms

His individuality is expressed in little ways with which all are familiar—his tie-ring, his gloves always stitched in black on the back, his trousers creased down the side following an old naval custom. Those who work with him know his insistence on order and punctuality, his knowledge of what he wants and his habit of getting it. There is the story of the well-meaning officious official and the King's quiet reply, accompanied by use of the waste-paper basket—"Now, Mr. So-and-so, if you don't mind, we will do it my way."

The traditional royal pageantry may warm us, or it may count for nothing : everything depends on the central figure. It is because all recognise, in his processional splendour and formality, the same wise leader, whose family life has set a standard for his reign, that the King is venerated as much in his State coach as in a circle of workmen.

When he was crowned the voices of the choir rose and filled Westminster Abbey with the noblest of exhortations— "Be strong and play the man : keep the commandments of the Lord Thy God, and walk in His ways."

All these things he has striven to do : and the measure of his success is in the loyal affection of his Peoples.

Copyright Reserved

to form a National Government : and, after a further conference with Mr. Baldwin and Sir Herbert Samuel, was able to declare its policy in the evening.

The Man who is King

It is plain sense to say that the essential stability of the British peoples is crystallised in the King whose Silver Jubilee is celebrated this year. The phrase made unforgettable by a cough in his Christmas Broadcast in 1934—"This is not spectacular work"—applies in very truth to the extraordinary growth in prestige of the monarchy for which he and the Queen have been responsible.

The King's impassivity—in other words his belief in the motto already quoted, "Keep Your Hair On !"—is part of a personality that is not so highly coloured as the sensationally minded could wish. But this comparative—and highly desirable—"colourlessness" is that of a great and impartial judge of men and affairs : this impassivity belongs to the supreme referee.

His Daily Round

His daily life is his daily work, for a King can never "hand over" to any one else. Despatches and messages pursue him from London to Windsor, from Windsor to Balmoral, from Balmoral to Sandringham, to his yacht and on country house visits and provincial tours. An infinitely elastic telephone line stretches after him everywhere. Before breakfast in Buckingham Palace he has begun his daily reading of as many newspapers as the average man gets through in a fortnight. Until lunch he works with his secretaries, dealing with the daily submission of State papers and his private correspondence. He will receive

"I am encouraged by the knowledge that I have in my dear wife one who will be a constant helpmate in every endeavour for our people's good"

God save Our King and Queen

PRINTED BY CLARKE & SHERWELL LTD., LONDON and NORTHAMPTON